C000003074

HINDU TALES

FROM THE SANSKRIT

HINDU TALES

FROM THE SANSKRIT

Translated by:
S.M. MITRA
Adapted by:
MR. ARTHUR BELL

MANOR
Rockville, MARYLAND
2008

Hindu Tales from the Sanskrit translated by S.M. Mitra in its current format, copyright © Arc Manor 2008. This book, in whole or in part, may not be copied or reproduced in its current format by any means, electronic, mechanical or otherwise without the permission of the publisher.

The original text has been reformatted for clarity and to fit this edition.

Arc Manor, Arc Manor Classic Reprints, Manor Classics, TARK Classic Fiction, and the Arc Manor and TARK Classic Fiction logos are trademarks or registered trademarks of Arc Manor Publishers, Rockville, Maryland. All other trademarks are properties of their respective owners.

This book is presented as is, without any warranties (implied or otherwise) as to the accuracy of the production, text or translation. The publisher does not take responsibility for any typesetting, formatting, translation or other errors which may have occurred during the production of this book.

ISBN: 978-1-60450-167-4

Published by Arc Manor
P. O. Box 10339
Rockville, MD 20849-0339
www.ArcManor.com

Printed in the United States of America/United Kingdom

Contents

INTRODUCTORY NOTE

Thanks to Mr. S. M. Mitra, the well-known Hindu psychologist and politician, who has done so much to draw more closely together the land of his birth and that of his adoption, I am able to bring within reach of English children a number of typical Hindu Tales, translated by him from the Sanskrit, some of them culled from the ancient classics of India, others from widely separated sources. The latter have hitherto been quite inaccessible to western students, as they are not yet embodied in literature, but have been transmitted orally from generation to generation for many centuries.

These tales are not only of a kind to enchain the attention of children. They also illustrate well the close affinity between the two chief branches of the great Aryan race, and are of considerable ethical value, reflecting, as they do, the philosophy of self-realisation which lies at the root of Hindu culture. They have been used from time immemorial by the best teachers of India as a means of building up the personalities of the young and maintaining the efficiency of the adult. They serve in fact as text-books of the unique system of Mind-Training which has been in use in India from remote Vedic times, the root principle of which is as simple as it is effective.

Hindu children become familiar at their mothers' knees with these stories, and are trained to answer questions on them, subtly chosen to suit their ages and call into action their mental faculties. Appealing to them as an amusing game, in which they vie with each other in trying to solve the problems presented for their consideration, the boys and girls, who are educated together till they are ten or twelve years old, early learn to concentrate their attention; whilst the simultaneous development of all their powers is encouraged and they are, imperceptibly to themselves led to control their thoughts and emotions from within, instead of having to obey orders which they do not understand from without. They realize indeed, whilst still in the nursery, the ideal suggested by the sage Vidura in the Mahabharata: "Seek to know thyself by means of thyself, keeping thy mind, intellect and senses, under control; for self is thy friend as it is also thy foe."

Nancy Bell.
Southbourne-on-Sea, 1918.

THE MAGIC PITCHER

CHAPTER I

Long, long ago there lived far away in India a woodcutter called Subha Datta and his family, who were all
very happy together. The father went every day to the forest near his home to get supplies of wood, which he sold
to his neighbours, earning by that means quite enough to
give his wife and children all that they needed. Sometimes
he took his three boys with him, and now and then, as a
special treat, his two little girls were allowed to trot along
beside him. The boys longed to be allowed to chop wood for
themselves, and their father told them that as soon as they
were old enough he would give each of them a little axe of
his own. The girls, he said, must be content with breaking
off small twigs from the branches he cut down, for he did
not wish them to chop their own fingers off. This will show
you what a kind father he was, and you will be very sorry for
him when you hear about his troubles.

All went well with Subha Datta for a long time. Each of
the boys had his own little axe at last, and each of the girls
had a little pair of scissors to cut off twigs; and very proud they
all were when they brought some wood home to their mother
to use in the house. One day, however, their father told them
they could none of them come with him, for he meant to go
a very long way into the forest, to see if he could find better
wood there than nearer home. Vainly the boys entreated him

to take them with him. "Not to-day," he said, "you would be too tired to go all the way, and would lose yourselves coming back alone. You must help your mother to-day and play with your sisters." They had to be content, for although Hindu children are as fond of asking questions as English boys and girls, they are very obedient to their parents and do all they are told without making any fuss about it.

Of course, they expected their father would come back the day he started for the depths of the forest, although they knew he would be late. What then was their surprise when darkness came and there was no sign of him! Again and again their mother went to the door to look for him, expecting every moment to see him coming along the beaten path which led to their door. Again and again she mistook the cry of some night-bird for his voice calling to her. She was obliged at last to go to bed with a heavy heart, fearing some wild beast had killed him and that she would never see him again.

CHAPTER II

When Subha Datta started for the forest, he fully intended to come back the same evening; but as he was busy cutting down a tree, he suddenly had a feeling that he was no longer alone. He looked up, and there, quite close to him, in a little clearing where the trees had been cut down by some other woodcutter, he saw four beautiful young girls looking like fairies in their thin summer dresses and with their long hair flowing down their backs, dancing round and round, holding each other's hands. Subha Datta was so astonished at the sight that he let his axe fall, and the noise startled the dancers, who all four stood still and stared at him.

The woodcutter could not say a word, but just gazed and gazed at them, till one of them said to him: "Who are you, and what are you doing in the very depths of the forest where we have never before seen a man?"

"I am only a poor woodcutter," he replied, "come to get some wood to sell, so as to give my wife and children something to eat and some clothes to wear."

"That is a very stupid thing to do," said one of the girls. "You can't get much money that way. If you will only stop with us we will have your wife and children looked after for you much better than you can do it yourself."

CHAPTER III

Subha Datta, though he certainly did love his wife and children, was so tempted at the idea of stopping in the forest with the beautiful girls that, after hesitating a little while, he said, "Yes, I will stop with you, if you are quite sure all will be well with my dear ones."

"You need not be afraid about that," said another of the girls. "We are fairies, you see, and we can do all sorts of wonderful things. It isn't even necessary for us to go where your dear ones are. We shall just wish them everything they want, and they will get it. And the first thing to be done is to give you some food. You must work for us in return, of course."

Subha Datta at once replied, "I will do anything you wish."

"Well, begin by sweeping away all the dead leaves from the clearing, and then we will all sit down and eat together."

Subha Datta was very glad that what he was asked to do was so easy. He began by cutting a branch from a tree, and with it he swept the floor of what was to be the dining-room. Then he looked about for the food, but he could see nothing but a great big pitcher standing in the shade of a tree, the branches of which hung over the clearing. So he said to one of the fairies, "Will you show me where the food is, and exactly where you would like me to set it out?"

At these questions all the fairies began to laugh, and the sound of their laughter was like the tinkling of a number of bells.

CHAPTER IV

When the fairies saw how astonished Subha Datta was at the way they laughed, it made them laugh still more, and they seized each other's hands again and whirled round and round, laughing all the time.

Poor Subha Datta, who was very tired and hungry, began to get unhappy and to wish he had gone straight home after all. He stooped down to pick up his axe, and was just about to turn away with it, when the fairies stopped their mad whirl and cried to him to stop. So he waited, and one of them said:

"We don't have to bother about fetching this and fetching that. You see that big pitcher. Well, we get all our food and everything else we want out of it. We just have to wish as we put our hands in, and there it is. It's a magic pitcher—the only one there is in the whole wide world. You get the food you would like to have first, and then we'll tell you what we want."

Subha Datta could hardly believe his ears when he heard that. Down he threw his axe, and hastened to put his hand in the pitcher, wishing for the food he was used to. He loved curried rice and milk, lentils, fruit and vegetables, and very soon he had a beautiful meal spread out for himself on the ground. Then the fairies called out, one after the other, what they wanted for food, things the woodcutter had never heard of or seen, which made him quite discontented with what he had chosen for himself.

CHAPTER V

The next few days passed away like a dream, and at first Subha Datta thought he had never been so happy in his life. The fairies often went off together leaving him alone, only coming back to the clearing when they wanted something out of the pitcher. The woodcutter got all kinds of things he fancied for himself, but presently he began to wish he had his wife and children with him to share his wonderful meals. He began to miss them terribly, and he missed his work too. It was no good cutting trees down and chopping up wood when all the food was ready cooked. Sometimes he thought he would slip off home when the fairies were away, but when he looked at the pitcher he could not bear the thought of leaving it.

CHAPTER VI

Soon Subha Datta could not sleep well for thinking of the wife and children he had deserted. Suppose they were hungry when he had plenty to eat! It even came into his head that he might steal the pitcher and take it home with him when the fairies were away. But he had not after all the courage to do this; for even when the beautiful girls were not in sight, he had a feeling that they would know if he tried to go off with the pitcher, and that they would be able to punish him in some terrible way. One night he had a dream that troubled him very much. He saw his wife sitting crying bitterly in the little home he used to love, holding the youngest child on her knee whilst the other three stood beside her looking at her very, very sadly. He started up from the ground on which he lay, determined to go home at once; but at a little distance off he saw the fairies dancing in the moonlight, and somehow he felt again he could not leave them and the pitcher. The next day, however, he was so miserable that the fairies noticed it, and one of them said to him: "Whatever is the matter? We don't care to keep unhappy people here. If you can't enjoy life as we do, you had better go home."

Then Subha Datta was very much frightened lest they should really send him away; so he told them about his dream and that he was afraid his dear ones were starving for want of the money lie used to earn for them.

"Don't worry about them," was the reply: "we will let your wife know what keeps you away. We will whisper in her ear when she is asleep, and she will be so glad to think of your happiness that she will forget her own troubles."

CHAPTER VII

Subha Datta was very much cheered by the sympathy of the fairies, so much so that he decided to stop with them for a little longer at least. Now and then he felt restless, but on the whole the time passed pleasantly, and the pitcher was a daily delight to him.

Meanwhile his poor wife was at her wits' end how to feed her dear children. If it had not been that the two boys were brave, plucky little chaps, she really would have been in despair. When their father did not come back and all their efforts to find him were in vain, these boys set to work to help their mother. They could not cut down trees, but they could climb them and chop off small branches with their axes; and this they did, making up bundles of faggots and selling them to their neighbours. These neighbours were touched by the courage they showed, and not only paid them well for the wood but often gave them milk and rice and other little things to help them. In time they actually got used to being without Subha Datta, and the little girls nearly forgot all about him. Little did they dream of the change that was soon to come into their lives.

CHAPTER VIII

A month passed peacefully away in the depths of the forest, Subha Datta waiting on the fairies and becoming every day more selfish and bent on enjoying himself. Then he had another dream, in which he saw his wife and children in the old home with plenty of food, and evidently so happy without him that he felt quite determined to go and show them he was still alive. When he woke he said to the fairies, "I will not stop with you any longer. I have had a good time here, but I am tired of this life away from my own people."

The fairies saw he was really in earnest this time, so they consented to let him go; but they were kind-hearted people and felt they ought to pay him in some way for all he had done for them. They consulted together, and then one of them told him they wished to make him a present before he went away, and they would give him whatever he asked for.

CHAPTER IX

Directly the woodcutter heard he could have anything he asked for, he cried, "I will have the magic pitcher."

You can just imagine what a shock this was to the fairies! You know, of course, that fairies always keep their word. If they could not persuade Subha Datta to choose something else, they would have to give him their beloved, their precious pitcher and would have to seek their food for themselves. They all tried all they could to persuade the woodcutter to choose something else. They took him to their own secret treasure-house, in an old, old tree with a hollow trunk, even the entrance to which no mortal had ever been allowed to see. They blindfolded him before they started, so that he could never reveal the way, and one of them led him by the hand, telling him where the steps going down from the tree began. When at last the bandage was taken from his eyes, he found himself in a lofty hall with an opening in the roof through which the light came. Piled up on the floor were sparkling stones worth a great deal of gold and silver money, and on the walls hung beautiful robes. Subha Datta was quite dazed with all lie saw, but he was only an ignorant woodcutter and did not realize the value of the jewels and clothes. So when the fairies, said to him, "Choose anything you like here and let us keep our pitcher," he shook his head and said: "No! no! no! The pitcher! I will have the pitcher!" One fairy after another picked up the rubies and diamonds and other precious stones and held them in the light, that the woodcutter might see how lovely they were; and when he still only shook his head, they got down the robes and tried to make him put one of them on. "No! the pitcher! the pitcher!" he said, and at last they had to give it up. They bound his eyes again and led him back to the clearing and the pitcher.

CHAPTER X

Even when they were all back again in the clearing the fairies did not quite give up hope of keeping their pitcher. This time they gave other reasons why Subha Datta should not have it. "It will break very easily," they told him, "and then it will be no good to you or any one else. But if you take some of the money, you can buy anything you like with it. If you take some of the jewels you can sell them for lots of money."

"No! no! no!" cried the woodcutter. "The pitcher! the pitcher! I will have the pitcher!"

"Very well then, take, the pitcher," they sadly answered, "and never let us see your face again!"

So Subha Datta took the pitcher, carrying it very, very carefully, lest he should drop it and break it before he got home. He did not think at all of what a cruel thing it was to take it away from the fairies, and leave them either to starve or to seek for food for themselves. The poor fairies watched him till he was out of sight, and then they began to weep and wring their hands. "He might at least have waited whilst we got some food out for a few days," one of them said. "He was too selfish to think of that," said another. "Come, let us forget all about him and go and look for some fruit."

So they all left off crying and went away hand in hand. Fairies do not want very much to eat. They can live on fruit and dew, and they never let anything make them sad for long at a time. They go out of this story now, but you need not be unhappy about them, because you may be very sure that they got no real harm from their generosity to Subha Datta in letting him take the pitcher.

CHAPTER XI

You can just imagine what a surprise it was to Subha Datta's wife and children when they saw him coming along the path leading to his home. He did not bring the pitcher with him, but had hidden it in a hollow tree in the wood near his cottage, for he did not mean any one to know that he had it. He told his wife that he had lost his way in the forest, and had been afraid he would never see her or his children again, but he said nothing about the fairies. When his wife asked him how he had got food, he told her a long story about the fruits he had found, and she believed all he said, and determined to make up to him now for all she thought he had suffered. When she called the little girls to come and help her get a nice meal for their father, Subha Datta said: "Oh, don't bother about that! I've brought something back with me. I'll go and fetch it, but no one is to come with me."

Subha Datta's wife was sorely disappointed at this, because she loved her husband so much that it was a joy to her to work for him. The children too wanted, of course, to go with their father, but he ordered them to stop where they were. He seized a big basket which was fall of fuel for the fire, tumbled all the wood in it on the floor, and went off alone to the pitcher. Very soon he was back again with his basket full of all sorts of good things, the very names of which his wife and children had no idea of. "There!" he cried; "what do you think of that? Am I not a clever father to have found all that in the forest? Those are the 'fruits' I meant when I told Mother about them."

CHAPTER XII

Life was now, of course, completely changed for the family in the forest. Subha Datta no longer went to cut wood to be sold, and the boys also left off doing so. Every day their father fetched food for them all, and the greatest desire of each one of the family was to find out where it came from. They never could do so, for Subha Datta managed to make them afraid to follow him when he went forth with his basket. The secret he kept from the wife to whom he used to tell everything soon began to spoil the happiness of the home. The children who had no longer anything to do quarrelled with each other. Their mother got sadder and sadder, and at last decided to tell Subha Datta that, unless he would let her know where the food came from, she would go away from him and take her little girls with her. She really did mean to do this, but something soon happened to change everything again. Of course, the neighbours in the wood, who had bought the fuel from the boys and helped them by giving them fruit and rice, heard of the return of their father and of the wonderful change in their lot. Now the whole family had plenty to eat every day, though none of them knew where it all came from. Subha Datta was very fond of showing off what he could do, and sometimes asked his old friends amongst the woodcutters to come and have a meal with him. When they arrived they would find all sorts of good things spread out on the ground and different kinds of wines in beautiful bottles.

This went on for some months, Subha Datta getting prouder and prouder of all that he could do, and it seemed likely that his secret would never be discovered. Everybody tried to find it out, and many followed him secretly when he set forth into the woods; but he was very clever at dodging them, hiding his treasure constantly in a new place in the dead of the night. If he had only been content with getting food out of his pitcher and drinking pure water, all would most likely have been well with him. But that was just what he could not do. Till he had his pitcher he had never drunk anything but water, but now he often took too much wine. It was this which led to the misfortune of losing his beloved pitcher. He began to boast of his cleverness, telling his friends there was nothing they wanted that he could not get for them; and one day when he had given them a very grand feast, in which were several rare kinds of food they had asked for, he drank too much wine—so much that he no longer knew what he was saying.

This was the chance his guests wanted. They began teasing him, telling him they believed he was really a wicked robber, who had stolen the food or the money to buy it. He got angry, and at last was actually silly enough to tell them all to come with him, and he would show them he was no robber. When his wife heard this, she was half pleased to think that now at last the secret would come out of where the food came from, and half afraid that something terrible would happen. The children too were greatly excited, and went with the rest of the party, who followed their father to the last hiding-place of the precious pitcher.

When, they all got very near the place, however, some idea began to come into Subha Datta's head that he was doing a very foolish thing. He stopped suddenly, turned round facing the crowd that followed him, and said he would not go a step further till they all went back to the cottage. His wife begged him to let her at least go with him, and the children all clamoured not to be sent back, but it was no good. Back they all had to go, the woodcutter watching till they were out of sight.

CHAPTER XIII

When the woodcutter was quite sure that every one was gone and nobody could see where he had hidden the pitcher, he took it from the hole in which it lay and carried it carefully to his home. You can imagine how everybody rushed out to meet him when he came in sight, and crowded round him, so that there was danger of the pitcher being thrown to the ground and broken. Subha Datta however managed to get into the cottage without any accident, and then he began to take things out of the pitcher and fling them on the ground, shouting, "Am I a robber? Am I a robber? Who dared to call me a robber?" Then, getting more and more excited, he picked up the pitcher, and holding it on his shoulder began to dance wildly about. His wife called out to him, "Oh, take care, take care! You will drop it!" But he paid no attention to her. Suddenly, however, he began to feel giddy and fell to the ground, dropping the pitcher as he did so. It was broken to pieces, and a great cry of sorrow went up from all who saw the accident. The woodcutter himself was broken-hearted, for he knew that he had done the mischief himself, and that if only he had resisted the temptation to drink the wine he would still have his treasure.

He was going to pick up the pieces to see if they could be stuck together, but to his very great surprise he could not touch them. He heard a silvery laugh, and what sounded like children clapping their hands, and he thought he also heard the words, "Our pitcher is ours again!" Could it all have been a dream? No: for there on the ground were the fruits and cakes that had been in the pitcher, and there were his wife, his children and his friends, all looking sadly and angrily at him. One by one the friends went away, leaving Subha Datta alone with his family.

CHAPTER XIV

This is the end of the story of the Magic Pitcher, but it was the beginning of a new chapter in the lives of Subha Datta and his family. They never forgot the wonder-working pitcher, and the children were never tired of hearing the story of how their father came to get it. They often wandered about in the forest, hoping that they too would meet with some wonderful adventure, but they never saw the fairies or found a magic pitcher. By slow degrees the woodcutter returned to his old ways, but he had learnt one lesson. He never again kept a secret from his wife; because he felt sure that, if he had told her the truth about the pitcher when he first came home, she would have helped him to save the precious treasure.

THE STORY OF
A CAT, A MOUSE,
A LIZARD AND AN OWL

CHAPTER I

This is the story of four creatures, none of whom loved each other, who lived in the same banyan tree in a forest in India. Banyan trees are very beautiful and very useful, and get their name from the fact that "banians," as merchants are called in India, often gather together in their shade to sell their goods. Banyan trees grow to a very great height, spreading their branches out so widely that many people can stand beneath them. From those branches roots spring forth, which, when they reach the ground, pierce it, and look like, columns holding up a roof. If you have never seen a banyan tree, you can easily find a picture of one in some dictionary; and when you have done so, you will understand that a great many creatures can live in one without seeing much of each other.

In an especially fine banyan tree, outside the walls of a town called Vidisa, a cat, an owl, a lizard and a mouse, had all taken up their abode. The cat lived in a big hole in the trunk some little distance from the ground, where she could sleep very cosily, curled up out of sight with her head resting on her forepaws, feeling perfectly safe from harm; for no other creature, she thought, could possibly discover her hiding-place. The owl roosted in a mass of foliage at the top of the tree, near the nest in which his wife had brought up their children, before those children flew away to seek mates for themselves. He too felt pretty secure as long as he remained up there; but he had seen the cat prowling about below him more than once, and was very sure that, if she should happen to catch sight of him when he was off his guard seeking his prey and obliged to give all his attention to what he was doing, she might spring out upon him and kill him. Cats do not generally attack such big birds as owls, but they will sometimes kill a mother sitting in her nest, as well as the little ones, if the father is too far off to protect them.

The lizard loved to lie and bask in the sunshine, catching the flies on which he lived, lying so still that they did not notice him, and darting out his long tongue suddenly to suck them into his mouth. Yet he hid from the owl and the cat, because he knew full well that, tough though he was, they would gobble him up if they happened to be hungry. He made his home amongst the roots on the south side of the tree where it was hottest, but the mouse had his hole on the other side amongst damp moss and dead leaves. The mouse was in constant fear of the cat and the owl. He knew that both of them could see in the dark, and he would have no chance of escape if they once caught sight of him.

CHAPTER II

The lizard and the mouse could only get food in daylight; but the lizard did not have to go far for the flies on which he lived, whilst the mouse had a very dangerous journey to take to his favourite feeding place. This was a barley field a short distance from the banyan tree, where he loved to nibble the full ears, running up the stalks to get at them. The mouse was the only one of the four creatures in the banyan tree who did not feed on others; for, like the rest of his family, he was a vegetarian, that is to say, he ate nothing but vegetables and fruit.

Now the cat knew full well how fond the mouse was of the barley-field, and she used to keep watch amongst the tall stems, creeping stealthily about with her tail in the air and her green eyes glistening, expecting any moment to see the poor little mouse darting hastily along. The cat never dreamt that any danger could come to her, and she trod down the barley, making quite a clear path through it. She was quite wrong in thinking herself so safe, for that path got her into very serious trouble.

It so happened that a hunter, whose great delight was to kill wild creatures, and who was very clever in finding them, noticing every little thing which could shew him where they had passed by, came one day into the barley-field. He spied the path directly and cried, "Ha! ha! Some wild animal has been here; not a very big one; let's have a look for the foot-prints!" So he stooped down to the ground, and very soon saw the marks of pussy's feet. "A cat, I do believe," he said to himself, "spoiling the barley she doesn't want to eat herself. I'll soon pay her out." The hunter waited until the evening lest the creature should see what he was going to do, and then in the twilight he set snares all over the barley-field. A snare, you know, is a string with a slip-knot at the end of it; and if an animal puts his head or one of his paws into this slip-knot and goes on without noticing it, the string is pulled tight and the poor creature cannot get free.

CHAPTER III

Exactly what the hunter expected happened. The cat came as usual to watch for the mouse, and caught sight of him running across the end of the path. Puss dashed after him; and just as she thought she really had got him this time, she found herself caught by the neck, for she had put her head into one of the snares. She was nearly strangled and could scarcely even mew. The mouse was so close that he heard the feeble mew, and in a terrible fright, thinking the cat was after him, he peeped through the stems of the barley to make sure which way to run to get away from her. What was his delight when he saw his enemy in such trouble and quite unable to do him any harm!

Now it so happened that the owl and the lizard were also in the barley-field, not very far away from the cat, and they too saw the distress their hated enemy was in. They also caught sight of the little mouse peeping through the barley; and the owl thought to himself, "I'll have you, my little friend, now puss cannot do me any harm," whilst the lizard darted away into the sunshine, feeling glad that the cat and the owl were neither of them now likely to trouble their heads about him. The owl flew quietly to a tree hard by to watch what would happen, feeling so sure of having the mouse for his dinner that he was in no hurry to catch him.

CHAPTER IV

The mouse, small and helpless though he was, was a wise little creature. He saw the owl fly up into the tree, and knew quite well that if he did not take care he would serve as dinner to that great strong bird. He knew too that, if he went within reach of the claws of the cat, he would suffer for it. "How I do wish," he thought to himself, "I could make friends with the cat, now she is in distress, and get her to promise not to hurt me if ever she gets free. As long as I am near the cat, the owl will not dare to come after me." As he thought and thought, his eyes got brighter and brighter, and at last he decided what he would do. He had, you see, kept his presence of mind; that is to say, he did not let his fright of the cat or the owl prevent him from thinking clearly. He now ventured forth from amongst the barley, and coming near enough to the cat for her to see him quite clearly, but not near enough for her to reach him with her claws, or far enough away for the owl to get him without danger from those terrible claws, he said to the cat in a queer little

S.M. MITRA

squeaky voice: "Dear Puss, I do not like to see you in such a fix. It is true we have never been exactly friends, but I have always looked up to you as a strong and noble enemy. If you will promise never to do me any harm, I will do my best to help you. I have very sharp teeth, and I might perhaps be able to nibble through the string round your beautiful neck and set you free. What do you think about it?"

CHAPTER V

When the cat heard what the mouse said, she could hardly believe her ears. She was of course ready to promise anything to anyone who would help her, so she said at once:

"You dear little mouse, to wish to help me. If only you will nibble through that string which is killing me, I promise that I will always love you, always be your friend, and however hungry I may be, I will starve rather than hurt your tender little body."

On hearing this, the mouse, without hesitating a moment, climbed up on to the cat's back, and cuddled down in the soft fur near her neck, feeling very safe and warm there. The owl would certainly not attack him there, he thought, and the cat could not possibly hurt him. It was one thing to pounce down on a defenceless little creature running on the ground amongst the barley, quite another to try and snatch him from the very neck of a cat.

The cat of course expected the mouse to begin to nibble through the string at once, and became very uneasy when she felt the little creature nestle down as if to go to sleep, instead of helping her. Poor Pussy could not turn her head so as to see the mouse without drawing the string tighter, and she did not dare to speak angrily lest she should offend him. "My dear little friend," she said, "do you not think it is high time to keep your promise and set me free?"

Hearing this, the mouse pretended to bite the string, but took care not to do so really; and the cat waited and

26

waited, getting more miserable every minute. All through the long night the same thing went on: the mouse taking a little nap now and then, the cat getting weaker and weaker. "Oh," she thought to herself, "if only I could get free, the first thing I would do would be to gobble up that horrid little mouse." The moon rose, the stars came out, the wind murmured amongst the branches of the banyan tree, making the unfortunate cat long to be safe in her cosy home in the trunk. The cries of the wild animals which prowl about at night seeking their food were heard, and the cat feared one of them might find her and kill her. A mother tiger perhaps would snatch her, and take her to her hungry cubs, hidden away in the deep forest, or a bird of prey might swoop down on her and grip her in his terrible claws. Again and again she entreated the mouse to be quick, promising that, if only he would set her at liberty, she would never, never, never forget it or do any harm to her beloved friend.

CHAPTER VI

It was not until the moon had set and the light of the dawn had put out that of the stars that the mouse, made any real effort to help the cat. By this time the hunter who had set the snare came to see if he had caught the cat; and the poor cat, seeing him in the distance, became so wild with terror that she nearly killed herself in the struggle to get away. "Keep still! keep still," cried the mouse, "and I will really save you." Then with a few quick bites with his sharp teeth he cut through the string, and the next moment the cat was hidden amongst the barley, and the mouse was running off in the opposite direction, determined to keep well out of sight of the creature he had kept in such misery for so many hours. Full well he knew that all the cat's promises would be forgotten, and that she would eat him up if she could catch him. The owl too flew away, and the lizard went off to hunt flies in the sunshine, and there was not a sign of any of the four inhabitants of the banyan tree when the hunter reached the snare. He was very much surprised and puzzled to find the string hanging loose in two pieces, and no sign of there having been anything caught in it, except two white hairs lying on the ground close to the trap. He had a good look round, and then went home without having found out anything.

When the hunter was quite out of sight, the cat came forth from the barley, and hastened back to her beloved home in the banyan tree. On her way there she spied the mouse also hurrying along in the same direction, and at first she felt inclined to hunt him and eat him then and there. On second thoughts however she decided to try and keep friends with him, because he might help her again if she got caught a second time. So she took no notice of the mouse until the next day, when she climbed down the tree and went to the roots in which she knew the mouse was hidden. There she began to purr as loud as she could, to show the mouse she was in a good humour, and called out, "Dear good little mouse, come out of your hole and let me tell you how very, very grateful I am to you for saving my life. There is nothing in the world I will not do for you, if you will only be friends with me."

The mouse only squeaked in answer to this speech, and took very good care not to show himself, till he was quite sure the cat was gone beyond reach of him. He stayed quietly in his hole, and only ventured forth after he had heard the cat climb up into the tree again. "It is all very well," thought the mouse, "to pretend to make friends with an enemy when that enemy is helpless, but I should indeed be a silly mouse to trust a cat when she is free to kill me."

The cat made a good many other efforts to be friends with the mouse, but they were all unsuccessful. In the end the owl caught the mouse, and the cat killed the lizard. The owl and the cat both lived for the rest of their lives in the banyan tree, and died in the end at a good old age.

STORY III

A ROYAL THIEF-CATCHER

CHAPTER I

In one of the smaller cities of India called Sravasti the people gathered together on a very hot day to stare at and talk about a stranger, who had come in to the town, looking very weary and walking with great difficulty because his feet were sore with tramping for a long distance on the rough roads. He was a Brahman, that is to say, a man who devoted his whole life to prayer, and had promised to give up everything for the sake of pleasing the god in whom he believed, and to care nothing for comfort, for riches, or for good food.

This Brahman carried nothing with him but a staff to help him along, and a bowl in which to receive the offerings of those who thought it their duty to help him and hoped by doing so to win favour in the sight of God. He was naked, except for a cloth worn about his loins, and his long hair was all matted together for want of combing and brushing. He made his way very slowly and painfully through the crowds, till he came to a shady corner, and there he sank down exhausted, holding out his bowl for the gifts of the people. Very soon his bowl would have been full of all sorts of good things, but he made it clear that he would accept nothing to eat except rice still in the husk, and nothing to drink but pure water. He was however willing to take money; and when the people who wished to help him found that out, they brought him a good many silver and gold pieces. Some who had no money to spare gave him jewels and other things which could be sold for money.

CHAPTER II

As time went on, the Brahman became very well known in Sravasti. His fame indeed spread far beyond the town, and people came from far away to consult him about all sorts of things, and he gave them good advice, for he was a very wise man. Those who wanted him to tell them what to do paid him for his advice, and as some of them had plenty of money and were glad to help him, he soon became quite rich. He might have done a great deal of good with all this money by helping the poor and suffering, but unfortunately he never thought of doing so. Instead of that, he got to love the money for its own sake. At night, when all those who had come to see him had gone to rest, and there was no fear of his being found out, he used to steal away into the forest, and there he dug a deep hole at the root of a great tree, to which he took all his money and jewels.

In India everybody has a siesta, that is to say, a sleep in the middle of the day, because the heat is so great it is difficult to keep well and strong without this extra rest. So, although it is quite light at the time, the streets are deserted, except for the dogs who prowl about, trying to find something to eat. Now the Brahman loved his money and other treasures so much, that he used very often to do without this siesta and go to the forest to enjoy the pleasure of looking at them. When he got to the tree, he would bend down, clear away the earth and leaves with which he had hidden his secret hole, take out the money and let it slip through his fingers, and hold up the jewels to the light, to watch how they gleamed and glistened. He was never so happy as when he was alone with his riches, and it was all he could do to tear himself away from them when the time came to go back to his shady corner. In fact he was becoming a selfish miser instead of the holy man the people of Sravasti thought he was. By the time the siesta was over he was always back again in his place beneath the tree, holding out his bowl and looking as poor and thin as ever, so that nobody had the least idea of the truth.

CHAPTER III

For many months the Brahman led this double life; until one day, when he went as usual to his hiding-place, he saw at once that some one had been there before him. Eagerly he knelt down, full of fear of exactly what had actually happened. All his care in concealing the hole had been wasted, for it was quite empty. The poor man could not at first believe his own eyes. He rubbed them hard, thinking that there was something the matter with them. Then he felt round and round the hole, hoping that after all he was mistaken; and when at last he was obliged to believe the terrible truth that there really was not a sign of his money and jewels, he became almost mad with misery. He began to run from tree to tree, peering into their roots, and when there was nothing to be seen, he rushed back again to his empty hole, to look into it once more. Then he wept and tore at his hair, stamped about and cried aloud to all the gods he believed in, making all kinds of promises, of what he would do if only they would give him back his treasures. No answer came, and he began to wonder who could have done such a terrible thing. It must, he felt sure, have been one of the people of Sravasti; and he now remembered he had noticed that a good many of them had looked into his bowl with longing eyes, when they saw the money and precious stones in it. "What horrible, wicked people they are," he said to himself. "I hate them. I should like to hurt them as they have hurt me." As he thought in this way he got more and more angry, until he became quite worn out with giving way to his rage.

CHAPTER IV

After roaming about in the forest for a long time, the Brahman went back to the house in Sravasti where some kind people had lent him a room, glad and proud to have such a holy man, as they thought he was, living under their roof. He felt sure they had had nothing to do with the loss of his treasure, because they had given him many proofs of their goodness and honesty. Soon he was pouring out all his grief to them, and they did all they could to comfort him, telling him that he would very soon have plenty more money and jewels. They let him see however that they thought it was mean of him to hide away his riches, instead of using them to help the poor and suffering; and this added very much to his rage. At last he lost all self-control and cried, "It is not worth while for me to live any longer. I will go to some holy place of pilgrimage by the banks of the river, and there I will starve myself to death."

A place of pilgrimage, you know, is one where some great event, generally connected with religion, has taken place, to which pilgrims go to pray in the hope of winning some special favour from God. The word pilgrim means a wanderer, but it has come in course of time to signify any traveller who comes from a distance to some such place. Benares in India is a very famous place of pilgrimage, because it is on the River Ganges, which the Hindus worship and love, believing that its waters can wash away their sins. Hundreds and thousands of Hindus go there every year to bathe in it, and many who know that they have not long to live wait on its banks to die, so that after their bodies have been burnt, as is the custom with the Hindus, their ashes may be thrown into the sacred stream.

CHAPTER V

The news of the Brahman's loss spread very quickly through Sravasti; and as is so often the case, every one who told the story made it a little different, so that it became very difficult to know what the truth really was. There was great distress in the town, because the people thought the Brahman would go away, and they did not want him to do that. They were proud of having a man they thought so holy, living amongst them, and ashamed that he should have been robbed whilst he was with them. When they heard that he meant to starve himself to death, they were dreadfully shocked, and determined to do all they possibly could to prevent it. One after another of the chief men of Sravasti came to see him, and entreated him not to be in such a hurry to be sure that his treasure would never be found. They said they would all do everything they possibly could to get it back for him. Some of them thought it was very wrong of him to make such a fuss about it, and blamed him for being a miser. They told him it was foolish to care so much for what he could not take with him when he died, and one specially wise old man gave him a long lecture on the wickedness of taking away the life which had been given to him by God to prepare for that in the other world. "Put the idea of starving yourself out of your head," he said, "and whilst we are seeking your treasure, go on as you did before you lost it. Next time you have any money and jewels, turn them to good account instead of hoarding them up."

CHAPTER VI

In spite of all that any one could say to him, the Brahman was quite determined that he would not live any longer. He set off to the place of pilgrimage he had chosen, taking no notice of any one he met, but just marching steadily on. At first a number of people followed him, but by degrees they left off doing so, and soon he was quite alone. Presently however he could not help noticing a man approaching from the direction in which he was going. Very tall, very handsome, very dignified, this man was one whom no one could fail to admire, even if he had been only an ordinary person. But he was the king of the whole country, whose name was Prasnajit; and a little distance behind him were a number of his attendants, waiting to obey his orders. Everybody, even the Brahman, loved the king, because he took such a very great interest in his people and was always trying to do them good. He had heard all about the loss of the money, and was very much vexed that such a thing should have happened in his land. He had also heard that the Brahman meant to kill himself, and this distressed him more than anything else, because he thought it a very wicked and terrible thing to do.

The king stood so exactly in the path of the Brahman that it was impossible to pass him by without taking any notice of him, and the unhappy man stood still, hanging down his head and looking very miserable. Without waiting for a moment, Prasnajit said to the Brahman: "Do not grieve any more. I will find your treasure for you, and give it back to you; or if I fail to do so I will pay you as much as it was worth out of my own purse: for I cannot bear to think of your killing yourself. Now tell me very carefully where you hid your gold and jewels, and everything about the place, to help me to make sure of it."

The Brahman was greatly delighted to hear this, because he knew full well that the king would keep his word, and that, even if his own treasure was never found, he would have plenty of money given to him by the king. He at once told Prasnajit exactly where he had put his store, and offered to take him there. The king agreed to go with him at once, and he and the Brahman went straight away to the big hole in the forest, the attendants following them a little way behind.

CHAPTER VII

After the king had seen the big empty hole, and noticed exactly where it was, and the nearest way to it from the town, he returned to his palace, first telling the Brahman to go back to the house he lived in, and wait there till he received a message from him. He promised to see that he wanted for nothing, and sent one of his attendants to a rich merchant of Sravasti, who had already done a good deal for the Brahman, to order him to supply the holy man with all he needed. Very glad that after all he was not going to die, the Brahman obeyed willingly, and for the next few days he was taken care of by the merchant, who supplied him with plenty of food.

As soon as Prasnajit was back in his palace, he pretended that he was taken suddenly ill. His head ached badly, he said, and he could not make out what was the matter with him. He ordered a proclamation to be sent all round the town, telling all the doctors to come to the palace to see him. All the doctors in the place at once hastened to obey, each of them hoping that he would be the one to cure the king and win a great reward. So many were they that the big reception room was full of them, and they all glared at each other so angrily that the attendants kept careful watch lest they should begin to fight. One at a time they were taken to the king's private room, but very much to their surprise and disappointment he seemed quite well and in no need of help from them. Instead of talking about his own illness, he asked each doctor who his patients were in the town, and what medicines he was giving to them. Of course Prasnajit's questions were carefully answered; but the king said nothing more, just waving his hand to shew that the interview was at an end. Then the attendants led the visitor out. At last however a doctor came, who said something which led the king to keep him longer than he had kept any of the others. This doctor was a very famous healer who had saved the lives of many of Prasnajit's subjects. He told the king that a merchant named Matri-Datta was very ill, suffering greatly, but that he hoped to cure him by giving him the juice of a certain plant called nagaballa. At the time this story was written, doctors in India did not give their patients medicine, or write prescriptions for them to take to chemists to be made up, because there were no chemists in those days, such as there are in all the towns of Europe, who keep the materials in stock for making medicines. A doctor just said to his patient, "you must take the juice of this or that plant"; and the suffering person had to go into the fields or woods to find the plant or else to send a servant to do so.

When the king heard that the doctor had ordered Matri-Datta to take the juice of the nagaballa plant, he cried "No more doctors need come to see me!" and after sending away the one who had told him what he wanted to know, he gave orders that Matri-Datta should be sent for at once.

CHAPTER VIII

Ill and suffering though he was, Matri-Datta did not dare disobey the king: so he came at once. As soon as he appeared, Prasnajit asked him how he was, and said he was sorry to have to make him leave his home when he was ill, but the matter on which he wished to see him was of very great importance. Then he suddenly added: "When your doctor ordered you to take the juice of the nagaballa plant whom did you send to find it?"

To this Matri-Datta replied trembling with fear: "My servant, O king, sought it in the forest; and having found it, brought it to me."

"Go back and send that servant to me immediately," was the reply; and the merchant hurried away, wondering very much why the king wanted to see the man, and hoping that he himself would not get into disgrace on account of anything he had done to make Prasnajit angry.

CHAPTER IX

When Matri-Datta told his servant that he was to go to the palace to see the king, the man was dreadfully frightened, and begged his master not to make him go. This made Matri-Datta pretty sure that he had done something wrong and was afraid of being found out. "Go at once," he said, "and whatever you do, speak the truth to the king. That will be your only chance if you have offended him." Again and again the servant entreated Matri-Datta not to insist, and when he found it was no good, he asked him at least to come with him to the palace and plead for him with Prasnajit. The merchant knew then for certain that something was seriously wrong, and he consented to go to the palace with his servant, partly out of curiosity and partly out of fear for himself. When the two got to the palace, the attendants at once led the servant to the presence of the king, but they would not let the master go with him.

Directly the servant entered the room and saw the king sitting on his throne, he fell upon his face at the foot of the steps, crying, "Mercy! mercy!" He was right to be afraid, for Prasnajit said to him in a loud voice: "Where are the gold and the jewels you took from the hole in the roots of a tree when you went to find the nagaballa plant for your master?" The servant, who really had taken the money and jewels, was so terrified when he found that the king knew the truth, that he had not a word to say at first, but just remained lying on the ground, trembling all over. Prasnajit too was silent, and the attendants waiting for orders behind the throne looked on, wondering what would happen now.

CHAPTER X

When the silence had lasted about ten minutes, the thief raised his head from the ground and looked at the king, who still said not a word. Something in his face however made the wicked servant hope that he would not be punished by death in spite of the great wrong he had done. The king looked very stern, it is true, but not enraged against him. So the servant rose to his feet, and clasping his hands together as he held them up to Prasnajit, said in a trembling voice: "I will fetch the treasure, I will fetch the treasure." "Go then at once," said the king, "and bring it here": and as he said it, there was a beautiful expression in his eyes, which made the thief more sorry for what he had done than he would have been if Prasnajit had said, "Off with his head!" or had ordered him to be beaten.

CHAPTER XI

As soon as the king said, "Go at once," the servant started to his feet and hastened away, as eager now to restore what he had stolen as he had been to hide it. He had put it in another hole in the very depths of the forest; and it was a long time before he got back to the palace with it, for it was very heavy. He had thought the king would send some guards with him, to see that he did not run away, and that they would have helped him to carry the sack full of gold and jewels; but nobody followed him. It was hard work to drag the heavy load all the way alone; but at last, quite late in the evening, he was back at the palace gates. The soldiers standing there let him pass without a word, and soon he was once more in the room in which the king had received him. Prasnajit still sat on his throne, and the attendants still waited behind him, when the thief, so tired he could hardly stand, once more lay prostrate at the bottom of the steps leading up to the throne, with the sack beside him. How his heart did beat as he waited for what the king would say! It seemed a very long time before Prasnajit spoke, though it was only two or three minutes; and when he did, this is what he said, "Go back to your home now, and be a thief no more."

Very, very thankfully the man obeyed, scarcely able to believe that he was free to go and that he was not to be terribly punished. Never again in the rest of his life did he take what did not belong to him, and he was never tired of telling his children and his friends of the goodness of the king who had forgiven him.

CHAPTER XII

The Brahman, who had spent the time of waiting in prayers that his treasure should be given back to him, and was still determined that, if it were not, he would starve himself to death, was full of delight when he heard that it had been found. He hastened to the palace and was taken before the king, who said to him: "There is your treasure. Take it away, and make a better use of it than before. If you lose it again, I shall not try to recover it for you."

The Brahman, glad as he was to have his money and jewels restored, did not like to be told by the king to make a better use of them. Besides this he wanted to have the thief punished; and he began talking about that, instead of thanking Prasnajit and promising to follow his advice. The king looked at him much as he had looked at the thief and said: "The matter is ended so far as I have anything to do with it: go in peace."

The Brahman, who was accustomed to be honoured by every one from the king on his throne to the beggars in the street, was astonished at the way in which Prasnajit spoke to him. He would have said more, but the king made a sign to his attendants, two of whom dragged the sack to the entrance of the palace and left it there, so that there was nothing for the Brahman to do but to take it away with him. Every one who has read this wonderful story would, of courses like to know what became of him after that, but nothing more is told about him.

STORY IV

THE MAGIC
SHOES AND STAFF

CHAPTER I

Far, far away in a town of India called Chinchini, where in days long gone by the ancient gods in whom the people believed are said sometimes to have appeared to those who called upon them for help, there lived three brothers of noble birth, who had never known what it was to want for food, or clothes, or a house to live in. Each was married to a wife he loved, and for many years they were all as happy as the day was long. Presently however a great misfortune in which they all shared befell their native country. There was no rain for many, many weeks; and this is a very serious thing in a hot country like India, because, when it does not rain for a long time, the ground becomes so parched and hard that nothing can grow in it. The sun is very much stronger in India than it is in England; and it sent forth its burning rays, drying up all the water in the tanks and changing what had been, a beautiful country, covered with green crops good for food, into a dreary desert, where neither men nor animals could get anything to eat. The result of this was that there was a terrible famine, in which hundreds of people and animals died, little children being the first to suffer.

Now the three brothers, who had none of them any children, got frightened at the state of things, and thought to themselves, "If we do not escape from this dreadful land, we shall die." They said to each other: "Let us flee away from here, and go somewhere where we are sure of being able to get plenty to eat and drink. We will not take our wives with us; they would only make things worse for us; let us leave them to look after themselves."

CHAPTER II

So the three wives were deserted, and had to manage as best they could without their husbands, who did not even trouble to wish them goodbye. The wives were at first very sad and lonely, but presently a great joy came to one of them which made the other two very happy as well. This joy was the birth of a little boy, whose two aunts loved him almost as much as his mother did. The story does not tell how they all got food whilst the famine was going on, though it is very evident that they were not starved, for the baby boy grew fast and was a strong healthy little fellow.

One night all the three wives had the same dream, a very wonderful one, in which the god Siva, who is very much honoured in India, appeared to them. He told them that, looking down from Heaven, he had noticed how tenderly they cared for the new-born baby, and that he wished them to call him Putraka. Besides this he astonished them by adding that, as a reward for the unselfish way in which they had behaved, they would find one hundred thousand gold pieces under the little child's pillow every morning, and that one day that little child would be a king.

CHAPTER III

The wonderful dream was fulfilled, and the mother and aunts called the boy Putraka. Every morning they found the gold pieces under his pillow, and they took care of the money for him, so that when he grew up he was the very richest man in the whole country. He had a happy child-hood and boyhood, his only trouble being that he did not like having never seen his father. His mother told him about the famine before he was born, and how his father and uncles had gone away and never come back. He often said, "When I am a man I will find my father and bring him home again." He used his money to help others, and one of the best things he did was to irrigate the land; that is to say, he made canals into which water was made to flow in times when there was plenty of rain, so that there was no danger of there being another famine, such as that which had driven his father and uncles away. The country in which he lived became very fruitful; everybody had enough to eat and drink; and Putraka was very much loved, especially by the poor and unhappy. When the king who ruled over the land died, everybody wanted Putraka to take his place, and he was chosen at once.

CHAPTER IV

One of the other wise things Putraka did, when he be-came king, was to make great friends with his Brahman subjects. Brahmans are always very fond of travelling, and Putraka thought, if he were good and generous to them, they would talk about him wherever they went, and that perhaps through them his father and uncles would hear about him. He felt sure that, if they knew he was now a king ruling over their native land, they would want to come back. He gave the Brahmans plenty of money, and told them to try and find his father and uncles. If they did, they were to say how anxious he was to see them, and promise them everything they wanted, if only they would return.

CHAPTER V

Just what the young king hoped came to pass. Wherever the Brahmans went they talked about the country they came from and the wonderful young king who ruled over it. Putraka's father and uncles, who were after all not so very far off, heard the stories about him, and asked the Brahmans many questions. The answers made them very eager to see Putraka, but they did not at first realize that he was closely related to them. Only when they heard the name of his mother did they guess the truth. Putraka's father knew, when he deserted his wife, that God was going to give her a child soon; which made it even more wicked of him to leave her. Now, however, he forgot all about that, only thinking how he could make as much use as possible of the son who had become a king. He wanted to go back at once alone, but the uncles were not going to allow that. They meant to get all they could out of Putraka too; and the three selfish men, who were now quite old, set off together for the land they had left so long ago.

They arrived safely, and made their way to the palace, where they were received, with great rejoicings. None of the wives, said a word of reproach to, the husbands who had deserted them; and as for Putraka, he was so over-joyed at having his father back, that he gave him a beautiful house to live in and a great deal of money. He was very good to his uncles too, and felt that he had now really nothing left to wish for.

CHAPTER VI

The three wives very soon had good reason to wish their husbands had stayed away. Instead of being grateful for all Putraka's generosity, they were very unkind and exacting, never pleased with anything; and whatever they had given them, they were always trying to get more. In fact, they were silly as well as wicked; for they did not realize that this was not the way to make the king love them or wish to keep them with him. Presently they became jealous of Putraka, and began to wish to get rid of him. His father hated to feel that his son was king, whilst he was only one of that king's subjects; and he made up his mind to kill him, hoping that if he could only get rid of him he might rule over the country in his stead. He thought and thought how best to manage this, and did not at first mean to tell his brothers anything about it; but in the end he decided he had better have them on his side. So he invited them to go with him to a secret place to talk the matter over.

CHAPTER VII

After many meetings the three wicked men decided that they would pay some one to kill the king, first making the murderer they chose swear that he would never tell who had ordered him to do the terrible deed. It was not very difficult to find a man bad enough to take money for such an evil purpose, and the next thing to do was to decide where and when the deed was to be done. Putraka had been very well brought up by his mother, and he often went to a beautiful temple near his palace to pray alone. He would sometimes stop there a long time, winning fresh wisdom and strength to do the work he was trusted with, and praying not only for himself, but for his father, his mother, his aunts and uncles, and for the people he loved so much.

The murderer was told to wait in this temple, and when the young king was absorbed in prayer, to fall suddenly upon him and kill him. Then, when Putraka was dead, he was to take his body and bury it far away in the depths of the forest where it could never be found. At first it seemed likely that this cruel plot would succeed.

To make quite sure, the murderer got two other men as wicked as himself to come and help him, promising to give them a share in the reward. But the god who had taken care of Putraka ever since he was born, did not forget him now. As the young king prayed, forgetting everything in his earnest pleading for those he loved, he did not see or hear the evil men drawing stealthily close to him. Their arms were uplifted to slay him, and the gleam of the weapons in the light that was always kept burning flashed upon him, when suddenly the heavenly guardian of the temple, who never left it day or night, but was generally invisible, appeared and cast a spell upon the wicked men, whose hands were arrested in the very act to strike.

What a wonderful sight that must have been, when Putraka, disturbed in his prayers, looked round and saw the men who had come to kill him, with the shadowy form of the guardian threatening them! He knew at once that he had been saved from a dreadful death by a messenger from the god he had been worshipping. As he gazed at the men, the guardian faded away and he was left alone with them. Slowly the spell cast on them was broken, and they dropped their weapons, prostrated themselves, and clasped their hands in an appeal for mercy to the man they had meant to destroy. Putraka looked at them quietly and sadly. He felt no anger against them, only a great thankfulness for his escape. He spoke to the men very sternly, asking them why they wished to harm him; and the chief murderer told him who had sent them.

The knowledge that his father wished to kill him shocked and grieved the young long terribly, but he controlled himself even when he learnt the sad truth. He told the men that he forgave them, for they were not the most to blame; and he made them promise never to betray who had bribed them to kill him. He then gave them some money and told them to leave him.

CHAPTER VIII

When Putraka was alone, he threw himself upon the ground and wept very bitterly. He felt that he could never be happy again, never trust anyone again. He had so loved his father and uncles. It had been such a joy to him to give them pleasure, and yet they hated him and wished to kill him. He wondered whether he was himself to blame for what had happened, and began to think he was not worthy to be king, if he could make such a mistake as he now feared he had made in being so generous to those who could have such hard thoughts of him as to want to take his life. Perhaps after all it would be better for his country to have another king. He did not feel as if he could go back to his palace and meet his father and uncles again. "What shall I do? What shall I do?" he cried, his sobs choking his voice. Never in all his life had he thought it possible to be so miserable as he was now. Everything seemed changed and he felt as if he were himself a different person. The only thing that comforted him at all was the thought of his mother, whose love had never failed him; but even that was spoiled by the remembrance that it was her husband who had wished to kill him. She must never know that, for it would break her heart: yet how could he keep it from her? Then the idea came to him that the best thing he could do would be to go away and never see his own people again.

CHAPTER IX

In the end the poor young king decided that he would go right away as his father and uncles had done; and his mind being made up, he became more cheerful and began to think he might meet with some interesting adventures in a new country, where nobody knew anything about him. As soon as it was light, he wandered off into the forest, feeling, it is true, very lonely, but at the same time taking a certain pleasure in being entirely his own master; which a king can never really be, because he has to consider so many other people and to keep so many rules.

After all Putraka did not find the forest so very lonely; for he had not gone far in it before his sad thoughts were broken in upon by his coming suddenly to a little clearing, where the trees had been cut down and two strong-looking men were wrestling together, the king watched them for a little while, wondering what they were fighting about. Then he called out, "What are you doing here? What are you quarrelling about?"

The men were greatly surprised to hear Putraka's voice, for they thought that they were quite alone. They stopped fighting for a minute or two, and one of them said: "We are fighting for three very precious things which were left behind him by our father."

"What are those things?" asked Putraka.

"A bowl, a stick and a pair of shoes," was the reply. "Whoever wins the fight will get them all. There they lie on the ground."

"Well, I never!" cried the king, laughing as he looked at the things, which seemed to him worth very little. "I shouldn't trouble to fight about such trifles, if I were you."

"Trifles!" exclaimed one of the men angrily. "You don't know what you are talking about. They are worth more than their weight in gold. Whoever gets the bowl will find plenty of food in it whenever he wants it; the owner of the stick has only to write his wishes on the ground with it and he will get them; and whoever puts on the shoes can fly through the air in them to any distance."

CHAPTER X

When Putraka heard the wonders which, could be done with what he had thought not worth having, he determined to get possession of the three treasures for himself; not considering that it would he very wrong to take what did not belong to him. "It seems a pity to fight," he said, "why don't you race for the things, and let whichever wins the race have them? That banyan tree over there would make a good winning post and I will be the umpire."

Instead of guessing what Putraka had in his mind, the brothers, who were very simple fellows, said at once: "All right. We won't fight, we'll race instead, and you can give us the start." Putraka agreed, and directly they were off he lost not a moment, but picked up the bowl and the staff, put on the shoes, and flew straight up into the air with the treasures. When the brothers came back, disputing about which of them had won, there was not a sign of Putraka, the bowl, the stick, or the shoes. They guessed at once what had happened; and after staring up in the air for a long time, they went home, feeling very much enraged with the man who had cheated them, and ashamed of having been so stupid as to trust him.

CHAPTER XI

On and on flew Putraka, full of eager delight in the new power of flight. How he loved rushing through the air, cleaving it like a bird on the wing! All he wanted to make him perfectly happy was someone to enjoy his new powers with him. Presently he found himself above a beautiful city with towers and pinnacles and minarets gleaming in the sunshine. "Ah!" he thought, "that is the place for me. I will go down there, and see if I can find a nice house to live in, and some people to make friends with, who will not try to kill me or to cheat me, but love me and be grateful to me for any kindness I show them."

As Putraka was hovering in the air above the town to which he had taken such a fancy, he noticed a little house which rather pleased him; for though it was poor-looking, there was something cheerful and home-like about it.

Down he sped and alighted at the door. Only one poor old woman lived in the house, and when Putraka knocked and asked if he might come in, she said "Yes" at once. He gave her some money, and told her he would like to live with her, if she would let him do so. She was only too glad to consent, for she was very lonely; and the two lived happily together for a long time.

CHAPTER XII

The old woman grew very fond of Putraka, caring for him and waiting on him as if he had been her own son. She was so anxious that he should be happy that she became afraid he would become tired of living alone with her. So she said to him one day: "My dear adopted son, you ought to have a wife to keep you company. I know the very one for you, the only one really worthy of you. She is a princess, and her name is Patala. She is so very lovely that every man who sees her falls in love with her and wants to carry her off. So she is most carefully guarded in the top rooms of a great palace, as high as the summits of the loftiest mountains." When Putraka heard this he was all eagerness to see the princess, and at once determined to go forth to seek her. He was more than ever glad now that he had stolen the shoes, because he knew that they would carry him even to the top of the highest mountains.

CHAPTER XIII

The very evening of the day when Putraka heard about the princess, he started on his journey, taking with him his bowl and staff. The old woman gave him very careful instructions which way to go, and begged him to come back to tell her how he had got on. He promised he would, thanked her for all she had done for him, and flew away in a great state of excitement. She watched him till he was quite out of sight, and then went sadly into her lonely home, wondering if she would ever see him again.

It was not long before Putraka came in sight of the palace. It was a beautiful night, and the moon was shining full upon the room in which the princess was asleep. It was a very big one, with costly furniture and priceless tapestry hung round the walls, and there were doors behind the tapestry leading to other apartments, in some of which the attendants on Patala slept, whilst others kept watch lest anyone should intrude upon their mistress. No one thought of guarding the windows, for they were so high up that only a bird could reach them.

The young king alighted on the ledge of the window of the princess' room, and looked in. There, on a golden bed, amongst soft cushions and embroidered coverings, lay the most lovely creature he had ever beheld, so lovely that he fell in love with her at once and gave a loud cry of delight. This woke the princess, who started up and was about to scream out aloud in her terror at seeing a man looking in at the window, when Putraka with the aid of his magic staff made himself invisible. Then, thinking she had been dreaming, Patala lay down again, and the king began talking to her in a low voice, telling her he had heard of her beauty and had flown from far away to see her. He begged her to allow him to show himself to her, and added: "I will go away again directly afterwards if you wish it."

Putraka's voice was so gentle, and it seemed to Patala so wonderful that a man could fly and make himself invisible, that she was full of curiosity to see him and find out all about him. So she gave her consent, and immediately afterwards the young king stood within the room, looking so noble and so handsome that she too fell in love at first sight. Putraka told her all about his life and adventures, which interested her very much. She was glad, she said, that he was a king; but she would have loved him just as well, whoever he might have been.

After a long talk, Patala begged him to leave her for fear her attendants should discover him and tell her father about him. "My father would never let me marry you," she declared, "unless you were to come with many followers as a king to ask my hand; and how can you do that when you are only a wandering exile?"

CHAPTER XIV

It was very difficult to persuade Putraka to go, but at last he flew away. Every night after that, however, he came to see Patala, spending the days sometimes in one place, sometimes in another, and using his magic bowl to supply himself with food. Alas, he forgot all about the dear old woman to whom he owed all his happiness, and she slowly gave up hope of ever seeing him again. He might quite easily have flown to her cottage and cheered her with his presence; but he was so wrapped up in his love for Patala that everything else went out of his head. This selfishness on his part presently got him into serious trouble, for he became careless about making himself invisible when he flew up to the princess' window. So that one night he was discovered by a guardian of the palace. The matter was at once reported to the king, who could not at first believe such a thing was possible. The man must have seen a big bird, that was all. The king, however, ordered one of his daughter's ladies to keep watch every night in an ante-room, leaving the door open with the tapestry, in which there was a slit, drawn carefully over it, and to come and tell him in the morning if she had seen or heard anything unusual.

Now the lady chosen loved the princess, and, like many of her fellow-attendants, thought it was very cruel of the king to punish his own child for being so beautiful, by shutting her up as he did. It so happened that the very first night she was on guard, Putraka had flown a very, very long way, not noticing where he was going, because he was thinking so earnestly of Patala. When at last he flew in at her window, he was so weary that he sank down on a couch and fell fast asleep. The princess too was tired, because she had lain awake talking to her lover so many nights running that she had had hardly any rest. So when the lady peeped through the slit in the tapestry, there, by the light of the night lamp, she saw the young king lying unconscious, whilst the princess also was asleep.

Very cautiously the attendant crept to the side of Putraka, and took a long, long look at him. She noticed how handsome he was, and that he was dressed in beautiful clothes. She especially remarked the turban he wore, because in India the rank to which men belong is shown by the kind of turbans they wear. "This is no common man," she thought, "but a prince or king in disguise. What shall I do now? I will not raise an alarm which might lead to this beautiful young lover being killed and the heart of my dear mistress broken."

CHAPTER XV

After hesitating a long time, the lady made up her mind that she would only put some mark in the turban of Putraka, so that he could be known again, and let him escape that night at least. So she stole back to her room, fetched a tiny, brooch, and fastened it in the folds of the turban, where the wearer was not likely to notice it himself. This done, she went back to listen at the door.

It was nearly morning when Putraka woke up, very much surprised at finding himself lying on the couch, for he did not remember throwing himself down on it. Starting up, he woke Patala, who was terribly frightened, for she expected her ladies to come in any minute to help her to dress. She entreated Putraka to make himself invisible and fly away at once. He did so; and, as usual, wandered about until the time should come to go back to the palace. But he still felt too tired to fly, and instead walked about in the town belonging to Patala's father.

The lady who had been on guard had half a mind to tell her mistress that her secret was discovered. But before she could get a chance to do so, she was sent for by the king, who asked her if she had seen or heard anything during the night. She tried very hard to escape from betraying Patala; but she hesitated so much in her answers that the king guessed there was something she wanted to hide, and told her, if she did not reveal the whole truth, he would have her head shaved and send her to prison. So she told how she had found a handsome man, beautifully dressed, fast asleep in Patala's room; but she did not believe her mistress knew anything about it, because she too was asleep.

The king was of course in a terrible rage, and the lady was afraid he would order her to be punished; but he only went on questioning her angrily about what the man was like, so that he might be found and brought before him. Then the lady confessed that she had put the brooch in the turban, comforting herself with the thought that, when the king saw Putraka and knew that Patala loved him, he might perhaps relent and let them be married.

When the king heard about the brooch, he was greatly pleased; and instead of ordering the lady to be punished, he told her that, when the man who had dared to approach his daughter was found, he would give her a great reward. He then sent forth hundreds of spies to hunt for the man with a brooch in his turban, and Putraka was very soon found, strolling quietly about in the market-place. He was so taken by surprise that, though he had his staff in his hand and his shoes and bowl in the pocket of his robes, he had no time to write his wishes with the staff, or to put on the shoes, so he was obliged to submit to be dragged to the palace. He did all he could to persuade those who had found him to let him go, telling them he was a king and would reward them well. They only laughed at him and dragged him along with them to the palace, where he was at once taken before the king, who was sitting on his throne, surrounded by his court, in a great hall lined with soldiers. The big windows were wide open; and noticing this, Putraka did not feel at all afraid, for he knew he had only to slip on his shoes and fly out of one of the windows, if he could not persuade the king to let him marry Patala. So he stood quietly at the foot of the throne, and looked bravely into the face of his dear one's father.

This only made the king more angry, and he began calling Putraka all manner of names and asking him how he dared to enter the room of his daughter. Putraka answered quietly that he loved Patala and wished to marry her. He was himself a king, and would give her all she had been used to. But it was all no good, for it only made the king more angry. He rose from his throne, and stretching out his hand, he cried:

"Let him be scourged and placed in close confinement!"

Then Putraka with his staff wrote rapidly on the ground his wish that no one should be able to touch him, and stooping down slipped on his magic shoes. The king, the courtiers and the soldiers all remained exactly as they were, staring at him in astonishment, as he rose up in the air and flew out of one of the windows. Straight away he sped to the palace of Patala and into her room, where she was pacing to and fro in an agony of anxiety about him; for she had heard of his having been taken prisoner and feared that her father would order him to be killed.

CHAPTER XVI

Great indeed was the delight of Patala when her beloved Putraka once more flew in at her window; but she was still trembling with fear for him and begged him to go away back to his own land as quickly as possible.

"I will not go without you," replied Putraka. "Wrap yourself up warmly, for it is cold flying through the air, and we will go away together, and your cruel father shall never see you again."

Patala wept at hearing this, for it seemed terrible to her to have to choose between the father she loved and Putraka. But in the end her lover got his own way, and just as those who were seeking him were heard approaching, he seized his dear one in his arms and flew off with her. He did not return to his own land even then, but directed his course to the Ganges, the grand and beautiful river which the people of India love and worship, calling it their Mother Ganga. By the banks of the sacred stream the lovers rested, and with the aid of his magic bowl Putraka soon had a good and delicious meal ready, which they both enjoyed very much. As they ate, they consulted together what they had better do now, and Patala, who was as clever as she was beautiful, said:

"Would it not be a good thing to build a new city in this lovely place? You could do it with your marvellous staff, could you not?"

"Why, of course, I could," said Putraka laughing. "Why didn't I think of it myself?" Very soon a wonderful town rose up, which the young king wished to be as much as possible like the home he had left, only larger and fuller of fine buildings than it. When the town was made, he wished it to be full of happy inhabitants, with temples in which they might worship, priests to teach them how to be good, markets in which food and all that was needed could be bought, tanks and rivulets full of pure water, soldiers and officers to defend the gates, elephants on which he and his wife could ride, everything in fact that the heart of man or woman could desire.

The first thing Putraka and Patala did after the rise of their own town, which they named Patali-Putra[1] after themselves, was to get married in accordance with the rites of their religion; and for many, many years they reigned wisely over their people, who loved them and their children with all their hearts. Amongst the attendants on those children was the old woman who had shown kindness to Putraka in his loneliness and trouble. For when he told Patala the story of his life, she reproached him for his neglect of one to whom he owed so much. She made him feel quite ashamed of himself, and he flew away and brought the dear old lady back with him, to her very great delight.

---

[1] The city which occupied the site of present Patna was known as Patali-Putra in the time of Alexander the Great.

STORY V

THE JEWELLED ARROW

CHAPTER I

In the city of Vardhamana in India there lived a powerful king named Vira-Bhuja, who, as was the custom in his native land, had many wives, each of whom had several sons. Of all his wives this king loved best the one named Guna-Vara, and of all his sons her youngest-born, called Sringa-Bhuja, was his favourite. Guna-Vara was not only very beautiful but very good. She was so patient that nothing could make her angry, so unselfish that she always thought of others before herself, and so wise that she was able to understand how others were feeling, however different their natures were from her own.

Sringa-Bhuja, the son of Guna-Vara, resembled his mother in her beauty and her unselfishness; he was also very strong and very clever, whilst his brothers were quite unlike him. They wanted to have everything their own way, and they were very jealous indeed of their father's love for him. They were always trying to do him harm, and though they often quarrelled amongst themselves, they would band together to try and hurt him.

It was very much the same with the king's wives. They hated Guna-Vara, because their husband loved her more than he did them, and they constantly came to him with stories they had made up of the wicked things she had done. Amongst other things they told the king that Guna-Vara did not really love him but cared more for some one else than she did for him. The most bitter of all against her was the wife called Ayasolekha, who was cunning enough to know what sort of tale the king was likely to believe. The very fact that Vira-Bhuja loved Guna-Vara so deeply made him more ready to think that perhaps after all she did not return his affection, and he longed to find out the truth. So he in his turn made up a story, thinking by its means to find out how she felt for him. He therefore went one day to her private apartments, and having sent all her attendants away, he told her he had some very sad news for her which he had heard from his chief astrologer. Astrologers, you know, are wise men, who are supposed to be able to read the secrets of the stars, and learn from them things which are hidden from ordinary human beings. Guna-Vara therefore did not doubt that what her husband was about to tell her was true, and she listened eagerly, her heart beating very fast in her fear that some trouble was coming to those she loved.

Great indeed was her sorrow and surprise, when Vira-Bhuja went on to say that the astrologer had told him that a terrible misfortune threatened him and his kingdom and the only way to prevent it was to shut Guna-Vara up in prison for the rest of her life. The poor queen could hardly believe that she had heard rightly. She knew she had done no wrong, and could not understand how putting her in prison could help anybody. She was quite sure that her husband loved her, and no words could have expressed her pain at the thought of being sent away from him and her dear son. Yet she made no resistance, not even asking Vira-Bhuja to let her see Sringa-Bhuja again. She just bowed her beautiful head and said: "Be it unto me as my Lord wills. If he wishes my death, I am ready to lay down my life."

This submission made the king feel even more unhappy than before. He longed to take his wife in his arms and tell her he would never let her go; and perhaps if she had looked at him then, he would have seen all her love for him in her eyes, but she remained perfectly still with bowed head, waiting to hear what her fate was to be. Then the thought entered Vira-Bhuja's mind: "She is afraid to look at me: what Ayasolekha said was true."

CHAPTER II

So the king summoned his guards and ordered them to take his wife to a strong prison and leave her there. She went with them without making any resistance, only turning once to look lovingly at her husband as she was led away. Vira-Bhuja returned to his own palace and had not been there very long when he got a message from Ayasolekha, begging him to give her an interview, for she had something of very great importance to tell him. The king consented at once, thinking to himself, "perhaps she has found out that what she told me about my dear Guna-Vara is not true."

Great then was his disappointment when the wicked woman told him she had discovered a plot against his life. The son of Guna-Vara and some of the chief men of the kingdom, she said, had agreed together to kill him, so that Sringa-Bhuja might reign in his stead. She and some of the other wives had overheard conversations between them, and were terrified lest their beloved Lord should be hurt. The young prince, she declared, had had some trouble in persuading the nobles to help him, but he had succeeded at last.

Vira-Bhuja simply could not believe this story, for he trusted his son as much as he loved him; and he sent the mischief maker away, telling her not to dare to enter his presence again. For all that he could not get the matter out of his head. He had Sringa-Bhuja carefully watched; and as nothing against him was found out, he was beginning to feel more easy in his mind, and even to think of going to see Guna-Vara in her prison to ask her to confide in him, when something happened which led him to fear that after all his dear son was not true to him. This was what made him uneasy. He had a wonderful arrow, set with precious jewels, which had been given to him by a magician, and had the power of hitting without fail whatever it was aimed at from however great a distance. The very day he had meant to visit his ill-treated wife, he missed this arrow from the place in which he kept it concealed. This distressed him very much; and after seeking it in vain, he summoned all those who were employed in the palace to his presence, and asked if any of them knew anything about the arrow. He promised that he would forgive any one who helped him to get it back, even if it were the thief himself; but added that, if it was not found in three days, he would have all the servants beaten until the one who had stolen it confessed.

CHAPTER III

Now the fact of the matter was that Ayasolekha, who had told the wicked story about Guna-Vara, knew where the king kept the arrow, had taken it to her private rooms, and had sent for her own sons and those of the other wives, all of whom hated Sringa-Bhuja, to tell them of a plot to get their brother into disgrace, "You know," she said to them, "how much better your father loves Sringa-Bhuja than he does any of you; and that, when be dies, he will leave the kingdom and all his money to him. Now I will help you to prevent this by getting rid of Sringa-Bhuja.

"You must have a great shooting match, in which your brother will be delighted to take part, for he is very proud of his skill with the bow and arrow. On the day of the match, I will send for him and give him the jewelled arrow belonging to your father to shoot with, telling him the king had said I might lend it to him. Your father will then think he stole it and order him to be killed."

The brothers were all delighted at what they thought a very clever scheme, and did just what Ayasolekha advised. When the day came, great crowds assembled to see the shooting at a large target set up near the palace. The king himself and all his court were watching the scene from the walls, and it was difficult for the guards to keep the course clear. The brothers, beginning at the eldest, all pretended to try and hit the target; but none of them really wished to succeed, because they thought that, when Sringa-Bhuja's turn came, as their father's youngest son, he would win the match with the jewelled arrow. Then the king would order him to be brought before him, and he would be condemned to death or imprisonment for life.

Now, as very often happens, something no one in the least expected upset the carefully planned plot. Just as Sringa-Bhuja was about to shoot at the target, a big crane flew on to the ground between him and it, so that it was impossible for him to take proper aim. The brothers, seeing the bird and anxious to shoot it for themselves, all began to clamour that they should be allowed to shoot again. Nobody made any objection, and Sringa-Bhuja stood aside, with the jewelled arrow in the bow, waiting to see what they would do, but feeling sure that he would be the one to kill the bird. Brother after brother tried, but the great creature still remained untouched, when a travelling mendicant stepped forward and cried aloud:

"That is no bird, but an evil magician who has taken that form to deceive you all. If he is not killed before he takes his own form again, he will bring misery and ruin upon this town and the surrounding country."

You know perhaps that mendicants or beggars in India are often holy men whose advice even kings are glad to listen to; so that, when everyone heard what this beggar said, there was great excitement and terror. For many were the stories told of the misfortunes Rakshas or evil magicians had brought on other cities. The brothers all wanted to try their luck once more, but the beggar checked them, saying:

"No, no. Where is your youngest brother Sringa-Bhuja? He alone will be able to save your homes, your wives and your children, from destruction,"

Then Sringa-Bhuja came forward; and as the sun flashed upon the jewels in the stolen arrow, revealing to the watching king that it was his own beloved son who had taken it, the young prince let it fly straight for the bird. It wounded but did not kill the crane, which flew off with the arrow sticking in its breast, the blood dripping from it in its flight, which became gradually slower and slower. At the sight of the bird going off with the precious jewelled arrow, the king was filled with rage, and sent orders that Sringa-Bhuja should be fetched to his presence immediately. But before the messengers reached him, he had started in pursuit of the bird, guided by the blood-drops on the ground.

CHAPTER IV

As Sringa-Bhuja sped along after the crane, the beggar made some strange signs in the air with the staff he used to help him along; and such clouds of dust arose that no one could see in which direction the young prince had gone. The brothers and Ayasolekha were very much dismayed at the way things had turned out, and greatly feared that the king's anger would vent itself on them, now that Sringa-Bhuja had disappeared. Vira-Bhuja did send for them, and asked them many questions; but they all kept the secret of how Sringa-Bhuja had got the arrow, and promised to do all they could to help to get it back. Again the king thought he would go and see the mother of his dear youngest son; but again something held him back, and poor Guna-Vara was left alone, no one ever going near her except the gaoler who took her her daily food. After trying everything possible to find out where Sringa-Bhuja had gone, the king began to show special favour to another of his sons; and as the months passed by, it seemed as if the young prince and the jewelled arrow were both forgotten.

Meanwhile Sringa-Bhuja travelled on and on in the track of the drops of blood, till he came to the outskirts of a fine forest, through which many beaten paths led to a very great city. He sat down to rest at the foot of a wide-spreading tree, and was gazing up at the towers and pinnacles of the town, rising far upwards towards the sky, when he had a feeling that he was no longer alone. He was right: for, coming slowly along one of the paths, was a lovely young girl, singing softly to herself in a beautiful voice. Her eyes were like those of a young doe, and her features were perfect in their form and expression, reminding Sringa-Bhuja of his mother, whom he was beginning to fear he would never see again.

When the young girl was quite close to him, he startled her by saying, "Can you tell me what is the name of this city?"

"Of course, I can," she replied, "for I live in it. It is called Dhuma-Pura, and it belongs to my father: he is a great magician named Agni-Sikha, who loves not strangers. Now tell me who you are and whence you come?"

Then Sringa-Bhuja told the maiden all about himself, and why he was wandering so far from home. The girl, whose name was Rupa-Sikha, listened very attentively; and when he came to the shooting of the crane, and how he had followed the bleeding bird in the hope of getting back his father's jewelled arrow, she began to tremble.

"Alas, alas!" she said. "The bird you shot was my father, who can take any form he chooses. He returned home but yesterday, and I drew the arrow from his wound and dressed the hurt myself. He gave me the jewelled arrow to keep, and I will never part with it. As for you, the sooner you depart the better; for my father never forgives, and he is so powerful that you would have no chance of escape if he knew you were here."

Hearing this, Sringa-Bhuja became very sad, not because he was afraid of Agni-Sikha, but because he knew that he already loved the fair maiden who stood beside him, and was resolved to make her his wife. She too felt drawn towards him and did not like to think of his going away. Besides this, she had much to fear from her father, who was as cruel as he was mighty, and had caused the death already of many lovers who had wished to marry her. She had never cared for any of them, and had been content to live without a husband, spending her life in wandering about near her home and winning the love of all who lived near her, even that of the wild creatures of the forest, who would none of them dream of hurting her. Often and often she stood between the wrath of her father and those he wished to injure; for, wicked as he was, he loved her and wanted her to be happy,

CHAPTER V

Rupa-Sikha did not take long to decide what was best for her to do. She said to the prince, "I will give you back your golden arrow, and you must make all possible haste out of our country before my father discovers you are here."

"No! no! no! a thousand times no!" cried the prince. "Now I have once seen you, I can never, never leave you. Can you not learn to love me and be my wife?" Then he fell prostrate at her feet, and looked up into her face so lovingly that she could not resist him. She bent down towards him, and the next moment they were clasped in each other's arms, quite forgetting all the dangers that threatened them. Rupa-Sikha was the first to remember her father, and drawing herself away from her lover, she said to him:

"Listen to me, and I will tell you what we must do. My father is a magician, it is true, but I am his daughter, and I inherit some of his powers. If only you will promise to do exactly as I tell you, I think I may be able to save you, and perhaps even become your wife. I am the youngest of a large family and my father's favourite. I will go and tell him that a great and mighty prince, hearing of his wonderful gifts, has come to our land to ask for an interview with him. Then I will tell him that I have seen you, fallen in love with you, and want to marry you. He will be flattered to think his fame has spread so far, and will want to see you, even if he refuses to let me be your wife. I will lead you to his presence and leave you with him alone. If you really love me, you will find the way to win his consent; but you must keep out of his sight till I have prepared the way for you. Come with me now, and I will show you a hiding-place."

Rupa-Sikha then led the prince far away into the depths of the forest, and showed him a large tree, the wide-spreading branches of which touched the ground, completely hiding the trunk, in which there was an opening large enough for a man to pass through. Steps cut in the inside of the trunk led down to a wide space underground; and there the magician's daughter told her lover to wait for her return. "Before I go," she said, "I will tell you my own password, which will save you from death if you should be discovered. It is LOTUS FLOWER; and everyone to whom you say it, will know that you are under my protection."

When Rupa-Sikha reached the palace she found her father in a very bad humour, because she had not been to ask how the wound in his breast was getting on. She did her best to make up for her neglect; and when she had dressed the wound very carefully, she prepared a dainty meal for her father with her own hands, waiting upon him herself whilst he ate it. All this pleased him, and he was in quite an amiable mood when she said to him:

"Now I must tell you that I too have had an adventure. As I was gathering herbs in the forest, I met a man I had never seen before, a tall handsome young fellow looking like a prince, who told me he was seeking the palace of a great and wonderful magician, of whose marvellous deeds he had heard. Who could that magician have been but you, my father?" She added, "I told him I was your daughter, and he entreated me to ask you to grant him an interview."

Agni-Sikha listened to all this without answering a word. He was pleased at this fresh proof that his fame had spread far and wide; but he guessed at once that Rupa-Sikha had not told him the whole truth. He waited for her to go on, and as she said no more, he suddenly turned angrily upon her and in a loud voice asked her:

"And what did my daughter answer?"

Then Rupa-Sikha knew that her secret had been discovered. And rising to her full height, she answered proudly, "I told him I would seek you and ask you to receive him. And now I will tell you, my father, that I have seen the only man I will ever marry; and if you forbid me to do so, I will take my own life, for I cannot live without him."

"Send for the man immediately," cried the magician, "and you shall hear my answer when he appears before me."

"I cannot send," replied Rupa-Sikha, "for none knows where I have left him; nor will I fetch him till you promise that no evil shall befall him."

At first Agni-Sikha laughed aloud and declared that he would do no such thing. But his daughter was as obstinate as he was; and finding that he could not get his own way unless he yielded to her, he said crossly:

"He shall keep his fine head on his shoulders, and leave the palace alive; but that is all I will say."

"But that is not enough," said Rupa-Sikha. "Say after me, Not a hair of his head shall be harmed, and I will treat him as an honoured guest, or your eyes will never rest on him."

At last the magician promised, thinking to himself that he would find some way of disposing of Sringa-Bhuja, if he did not fancy him for a son-in-law. The words she wanted to hear were hardly out of her father's mouth before Rupa-Sikha sped away, as if on the wings of the wind, full of hope that all would be well. She found her lover anxiously awaiting her, and quickly explained how matters stood. "You had better say nothing about me to my father at first," she said; "but only talk about him and all you have heard of him. If only you could get him to like you and want to keep you with him, it would help us very much. Then you could pretend that you must go back to your own land; and rather than allow you to do so, he will be anxious for us to be married and to live here with him."

CHAPTER VI

Sringa-Bhuja loved Rupa-Sikha so much that he was ready to obey her in whatever she asked. So he at once went with her to the palace. On every side he saw signs of the strength and power of the magician. Each gate was guarded by tall soldiers in shining armour, who saluted Rupa-Sikha but scowled fiercely at him. He knew full well that, if he had tried to pass alone, they would have prevented him from doing so. At last the two came to the great hall, where the magician was walking backwards and forwards, working himself into a rage at being kept waiting. Directly he looked at the prince, he knew him for the man who had shot the jewelled arrow at him when he had taken the form of a crane, and he determined that he would be revenged. He was too cunning to let Sringa-Bhuja guess that he knew him, and pretended to be very glad to see him. He even went so far as to say that he had long wished to find a prince worthy to wed his youngest and favourite daughter. "You," he added, "seem to me the very man, young, handsome and—to judge from the richness of your dress and jewels—able to give my beloved one all she needs."

The prince could hardly believe his ears, and Rupa-Sikha also was very much surprised. She guessed however that her father had some evil purpose in what he said, and looked earnestly at Sringa-Bhuja in the hope of making him understand. But the prince was so overjoyed at the thought that she was to be his wife that he noticed nothing. So when Agni-Sikha added, "I only make one condition: you must promise that you will never disobey my commands, but do whatever I tell you without a moment's hesitation," Sringa-Bhuja, without waiting to think, said at once, "Only give me your daughter and I will serve you in any way you wish."

"That's settled then!" cried the magician, and he clapped his hands together. In a moment a number of attendants appeared, and their master ordered them to lead the prince to the best apartments in the palace, to prepare a bath for him, and do everything he asked them.

CHAPTER VII

As Sringa-Bhuja followed the servants, Rupa-Sikha managed to whisper to him, "Beware! await a message from me!" When he had bathed and was arraying himself in fresh garments provided by his host, waited on, hand and foot, by servants who treated him with the greatest respect, a messenger arrived, bearing a sealed letter which he reverently handed to the prince. Sringa-Bhuja guessed at once from whom it came; and anxious to read it alone, he hastily finished his toilette and dismissed the attendants.

"My beloved," said the letter—which was, of course, from Rupa-Sikha—"My father is plotting against you; and very foolish were you to promise you would obey him in all things. I have ten sisters all exactly like me, all wearing dresses and necklaces which are exact copies of each other, so that few can tell me from the others, Soon you will be sent for to the great Hall and we shall all be together there. My father will bid you choose your bride from amongst us; and if you make a mistake all will be over for us. But I will wear my necklace on my head instead of round my neck, and thus will you know your own true love. And remember, my dearest, to obey no future command without hearing from me, for I alone am able to outwit my terrible father,"

Everything happened exactly as Rupa-Sikha described. The prince was sent for by Agni-Sikha, who, as soon as he appeared, gave him a garland of flowers and told him to place it round the neck of the maiden who was his promised bride. Without a moment's hesitation Sringa-Bhuja picked out the right sister; and the magician, though inwardly enraged, pretended to be so delighted at this proof of a lover's clear-sightedness that he cried:

"You are the son-in-law for me! The wedding shall take place to-morrow!"

CHAPTER VIII

When Sringa-Bhuja heard what Agni-Sikha said, he was full of joy; but Rupa-Sikha knew well that her father did not mean a word of it. She waited quietly beside her lover, till the magician bade all the sisters but herself leave the hall. Then the magician, with a very wicked look on his face, said:

"Before the ceremony there is just one little thing you must do for me, dear son-in-law that is to be. Go outside the town, and near the most westerly tower you will find a team of oxen and a plough awaiting you. Close to them is a pile of three hundred bushels of sesame seed. This you must sow this very day, or instead of a bridegroom you will be a dead man to-morrow."

Great was the dismay of Sringa-Bhuja when he heard this. But Rupa-Sikha whispered to him, "Fear not, for I will help you." Sadly the prince left the palace alone, to seek the field outside the city; the guards, who knew he was the accepted lover of their favourite mistress, letting him pass unhindered. There, sure enough, near the western tower were the oxen, the plough and a great pile of seed. Never before had poor Sringa-Bhuja had to work for himself, but his great love for Rupa-Sikha made him determine to do his best. So he was about to begin to guide the oxen across the field, when, behold, all was suddenly changed. Instead of an unploughed tract of land, covered with weeds, was a field with rows and rows of regular furrows. The piles of seed were gone, and flocks of birds were gathering in the hope of securing some of it as it lay in the furrows.

As Sringa-Bhuja was staring in amazement at this beautiful scene, he saw Rupa-Sikha, looking more lovely than ever, coming towards him. "Not in vain," she said to him, "am I my father's daughter. I too know how to compel even nature to do my will; but the danger is not over yet. Go quickly back to the palace, and tell Agni-Sikha that his wishes are fulfilled."

CHAPTER IX

The magician was very angry indeed when he heard that the field was ploughed and the seed sown. He knew at once that some magic had been at work, and suspected that Rupa-Sikha was the cause of his disappointment. Without a moment's hesitation he said to the prince: "No sooner were you gone than I decided not to have that seed sown. Go back at once, and pile it up where it was before."

This time Sringa-Bhuja felt no fear or hesitation, for he was sure of the power and will to help him of his promised bride. So back he went to the field, and there he found the whole vast space covered with millions and millions of ants, busily collecting the seed and piling it up against the wall of the town. Again Rupa-Sikha came to cheer him, and again she warned him that their trials were not yet over. She feared, she said, that her father might prove stronger than herself; for he had many allies at neighbouring courts ready to help him in his evil purposes. "Whatever else he orders you to do, you must see me before you leave the palace. I will send my faithful messenger to appoint a meeting in some secret place."

Agni-Sikha was not much surprised when the prince told him that his last order had been obeyed, and thought to himself, "I must get this tiresome fellow out of my domain, where that too clever child of mine will not be able to help him." "Well," he said, "I suppose the wedding must take place to-morrow after all, for I am a man of my word. We must now set about inviting the guests. You shall have the pleasure of doing this yourself: then my friends will know beforehand what a handsome young son-in-law I shall have. The first person to summon to the wedding is my brother Dhuma Sikha, who has taken up his abode in a deserted temple a few miles from here. You must ride at once to that temple, rein up your steed opposite it, and cry, 'Dhuma Sikha, your brother Agni-Sikha has sent me hither to invite you to witness my marriage with his daughter Rupa-Sikha to-morrow. Come without delay!' Your message given, ride back to me; and I will tell you what farther tasks you must perform before the happy morrow dawns."

When Sringa-Bhuja left the palace, he knew not where to seek a horse to bear him on this new errand. But as he was nearing the gateway by which he had gone forth to sow the field with seed, a handsome boy approached him and said, "If my lord will follow me, I will tell him what to do." Somehow the voice sounded familiar; and when the guards were left far enough behind to be out of hearing, the boy looked up at Sringa-Bhuja with a smile that revealed Rupa-Sikha herself. "Come with me," she said; and taking his hand, she led him to a tree beneath which stood a noble horse, richly caparisoned, which pawed the ground and whinnied to its mistress, as she drew near.

"You must ride this horse," said Rupa-Sikha, "who will obey you if you but whisper in his ear; and you must take earth, water, wood and fire with you, which I will give you. You must go straight to the temple, and when you have called out your message, turn without a moment's delay, and ride for your life as swiftly as your steed will go, looking behind you all the time. No guidance will be necessary; for Marut—that is my horse's name—knows well what he has to do."

Then Rupa-Sikha gave Sringa-Bhuja a bowl of earth, a jar of water, a bundle of thorns and a brazier full of burning charcoal, hanging them by strong thongs upon the front of his saddle so that he could reach them easily. "My father," she told him, "has given my uncle instructions to kill you, and he will follow you upon his swift Arab steed. When you hear him behind you, fling earth in his path; if that does not stop him, pour out some of the water; and if he still perseveres, scatter the burning charcoal before him."

CHAPTER X

Away went the prince after he had received these instructions; and very soon he found himself opposite the temple, with the images of three of the gods worshipped in India to prove that it had been a sanctuary before the magician took up his abode in it. Directly Sringa-Bhuja shouted out his message to Dhuma-Sikha, the wicked dweller in the temple came rushing forth from the gateway, mounted on a huge horse, which seemed to be belching forth flames from its nostrils as it bounded along. For one terrible moment Sringa-Bhuja feared that he was lost; but Marut, putting forth all his strength, kept a little in advance of the enemy, giving the prince time to scatter earth behind him. Immediately a great mountain rose up, barring the road, and Sringa-Bhuja felt that he was saved. He was mistaken: for, as he looked back, he saw Dhuma-Sikha coming over the top of the mountain. The next moment the magician was close upon him. So he emptied his bowl of water: and, behold, a huge river with great waves hid pursuer and pursued from each other. Even this did not stop the mighty Arab horse, which swam rapidly across, the rider loudly shouting out orders to the prince to stop. When the prince heard the hoofs striking on the dry ground behind him again, he threw out the thorns, and a dense wood sprouted up as if by magic, which for a few moments gave fresh hope of safety to Sringa-Bhuja; for it seemed as if even the powerful magician would be unable to get through it. He did succeed however; but his clothes were nearly torn off his back, and his horse was bleeding from many wounds made by the cruel thorns. Sringa-Bhuja too was getting weary, and remembered that he had only one more chance of checking his relentless enemy. He could almost feel the breath of the panting steed as it drew near; and with a loud cry to his beloved Rupa-Sikha, he threw the burning charcoal on the road. In an instant the grass by the wayside, the trees overshadowing it, and the magic wood which had sprung from the thorns, were alight, burning so fiercely that no living thing could approach them safely. The wicked magician was beaten at last, and was soon himself fleeing away, as fast as he could, with the flames following after him as if they were eager to consume him.

Whether his enemy ever got back to his temple, Sringa-Bhuja never knew. Exhausted with all he had been through, the young prince was taken back to the palace by the faithful Marut, and there he found his dear Rupa-Sikha awaiting him. She told him that her father had promised her that, if the prince came back, he would oppose her marriage no longer. "For," he said, "if he can escape your uncle, he must be more than mortal, and worthy even of my daughter." "He does not in the least expect to see you again," added Rupa-Sikha; "and even if he allows us to marry, he will never cease to hate you; for I am quite sure he knows that you shot the jewelled arrow at him when he was in the form of a crane. If I ever am your wife, he will try to punish you through me. But have no fear: I shall know how to manage him. Fresh powers have been lately given to me by another uncle whose magic is stronger than that of any of my other relations."

When Sringa-Bhuja had bathed and rested, he robed himself once more in the garments he had worn the day he first saw Rupa-Sikha; and together the lovers went to the great hall to seek an interview with Agni-Sikha. The magician, who had made quite sure that he had now got rid of the unwelcome suitor for his daughter's hand, could not contain his rage, at seeing him walk in with her as if the two were already wedded.

He stamped about, pouring out abuse, until he had quite exhausted himself, the lovers looking on quietly without speaking. At last, coming close to them, Agni-Sikha shouted, in a loud harsh voice: "So you have not obeyed my orders. You have not bid my brother to the wedding. Your life is forfeit, and you will die to-morrow instead of marrying Rupa-Sikha. Describe the temple in which Dhuma Sikha lives and the appearance of its owner."

Then Sringa-Bhuja gave such an exact account of the temple, naming the gods whose images still adorned it, and of the terrible man riding the noble steed who had pursued him, that the magician was convinced against his will; and knowing that he must keep his word to Rupa-Sikha, he gave his consent for the preparations for the marriage on the morrow to begin.

CHAPTER XI

The marriage was celebrated the next day with very great pomp; and a beautiful suite of rooms was given to the bride and bridegroom, who could not in spite of this feel safe or happy, because they knew full well that Agni-Sikha hated them. The prince soon began to feel home-sick and anxious to introduce his beautiful wife to his own people. He remembered that he had left his dear mother in prison, and reproached himself for having forgotten her for so long. So he said to Rupa-Sikha:

"Let us go, beloved, to my native city, Vardhamana. My heart yearns after my dear ones there, and I would fain introduce you to them."

"My lord," replied Rupa-Sikha, "I will go with you whither you will, were it even to the ends of the earth. But we must not let my father guess we mean to go; for he would forbid us to leave the country and set spies to watch our every movement. We will steal away secretly, riding together on my faithful Marut and taking with us only what we can carry." "And my jewelled arrow," said the prince, "that I may give it back to my father and explain to him how I lost it. Then shall I be restored to his favour, and maybe he will forgive my mother also."

"Have no fear," answered Rupa-Sikha: "all will surely go well with us. Forget not that new powers have been given to me, which will save us from my father and aid me to rescue my dear one's mother from her evil fate."

Before the dawn broke on the next day, the two set forth unattended, Marut seeming to take pride in his double burden and bearing them along so swiftly that they had all but reached the bounds of the country under the dominion of Agni-Sikha as the sun rose. Just as they thought they were safe from pursuit, they heard a loud rushing noise behind; and looking round, they saw the father of the bride close upon them on his Arab steed, with sword uplifted in his hand to strike. "Fear not," whispered Rupa-Sikha to her husband. "I will show you now what I can do." And waving her arms to and fro, as she muttered some strange words, she changed herself into an old woman and Sringa-Bhuja into an old man, whilst Marut became a great pile of wood by the road-side.

When the angry father reached the spot, the bride and bridegroom were busily gathering sticks to add to the pile, seemingly too absorbed in their work to take any notice of the angry magician, who shouted out to them:

"Have you seen a man and a woman pass along this way?"

The old woman straightened herself, and peering, up into his face, said:

"No; we are too busy over our work to notice anything else."

"And what, pray, are you doing in my wood?" asked Agni-Sikha.

"We are helping to collect the fuel for the pyre of the great magician Agni-Sikha." answered Rupa-Sikha. "Do you not know that he died yesterday?"

The Hindus of India do not bury but burn the dead; so that it was quite a natural thing for the people of the land over which the magician ruled to collect the materials for the pyre or heap of wood on which his body would be laid to be burnt. What surprised Agni-Sikha, and in fact nearly took his breath away, was to be quietly told that he was dead. He began to think that he was dreaming, and said to himself, "I cannot really be dead without knowing it, so I must be asleep." And he quietly turned his horse round and rode slowly home again. This was just what his daughter wanted; and as soon as he was out of sight, she turned herself, her husband and Marut, into their natural forms again, laughing merrily, as she did so, at the thought of the ease with which she had got rid of her father.

CHAPTER XII

Once more the bride and bridegroom set forth on their way, and once more they soon heard Agni-Sikha coming after them. For when he got back to his palace, and the servants hastened out to take his horse, he guessed that a trick had been played on him. He did not even dismount, but just turned his horse's head round and galloped back again. "If ever," he thought to himself, "I catch those two young people, I'll make them wish they had obeyed me. Yes, they shall suffer for it. I am not going to stand being defied like this."

This time Rupa-Sikha contented herself with making her husband and Marut invisible, whilst she changed herself into a letter-carrier, hurrying along the road as if not a moment was to be lost. She took no notice of her father, till he reined up his steed and shouted to her:

"Have you seen a man and woman on horseback pass by?"

"No, indeed," she said: "I have a very important letter to deliver, and could think of nothing but making all the haste possible."

"And what is this important letter about?" asked Agni-Sikha. "Can you tell me that?"

"Oh, yes, I can tell you that," she said. "But where can you have been, not to have heard the terrible news about the ruler of this land?"

"You can't tell me anything I don't know about him," answered the magician, "for he is my greatest friend."

"Then you know that he is dying from a wound he got in a battle with his enemies only yesterday. I am to take this letter to his brother Dhuma-Sikha, bidding him come to see him before the end."

Again Agni-Sikha wondered if he were dreaming, or if he were under some strange spell and did not really know who he was? Being able, as he was, to cast spells on other people, he was ready to fancy the same thing had befallen him. He said nothing when he heard that he was wounded, and was about to turn back again when Rupa-Sikha said to him:

"As you are on horseback and can get to Dhuma-Sikha's temple quicker than I can, will you carry the message of his brother's approaching death to him for me, and bid him make all possible haste if he would see him alive?"

This was altogether too much for the magician, who became sure that there was something very wrong about him. He knew he was not wounded or dying, but he thought he must be ill of fever, fancying he heard what he did not. He stared fixedly at his daughter, and she stared up at him, half-afraid he might find out who she was, but he never guessed.

"Do your own errands," he said at last; and slashing his poor innocent horse with his whip, he wheeled round and dashed home again as fast as he could. Again his servants ran out to receive him, and he gloomily dismounted, telling them to send his chief councillor to him in his private apartments. Shut up with him, he poured out all his troubles, and the councillor advised him to see his physician without any delay, for he felt sure that these strange fancies were caused by illness.

The doctor, when he came, was very much puzzled, but he looked as wise as he could, ordered perfect rest and all manner of disagreeable medicines. He was very much surprised at the change he noticed in his patient, who, instead of angrily declaring that there was nothing the matter with him, was evidently in a great fright about his health. He shut himself up for many days, and it was a long time before he got over the shock he had received, and then it was too late for him to be revenged or the lovers.

CHAPTER XIII

Having really got rid of Agni-Sikha, Rupa-Sikha and her husband were very soon out of his reach and in the country belonging to Sringa-Bhuja's father, who had bitterly mourned the loss of his favourite son. When the news was brought to him that two strangers, a handsome young man and a beautiful woman, who appeared to be husband and wife, had entered his capital, he hastened forth to meet them, hoping that perhaps they could give him news of Sringa-Bhuja. What was his joy when he recognised his dear son, holding the jewelled arrow, which had led him into such trouble, in his right hand, as he guided Marat with his left! The king flung himself from his horse, and Sringa-Bhuja, giving the reins to Rupa-Sikha, also dismounted. The next moment he was in his father's arms, everything forgotten and forgiven in the happy reunion.

Great was the rejoicing over Sringa-Bhuja's return and hearty was the welcome given to his beautiful bride, who quickly won all hearts but those of the wicked wives and sons who had tried to harm her husband and his mother.

They feared the anger of the king, when he found out how they had deceived him, and they were right to fear. Sringa-Bhuja's very first act was to plead for his mother to be set free. He would not tell any of his adventures, he said, till she could hear them too; and the king, full of remorse for the way he had treated her, went with him to the prison in which she had been shut up all this time. What was poor Guna-Vara's joy, when the two entered the place in which she had shed so many tears! She could not at first believe her eyes or ears, but soon she realised that her sufferings were indeed over. She could not be quite happy till her beloved husband said he knew she had never loved any one but him. She had been accused falsely, she said, and she wanted the woman who had told a lie about her to be made to own the truth.

This was done in the presence of the whole court, and when judgment had been passed upon Ayasolekha, the brothers of Sringa-Bhuja were also brought before their father, who charged them with having deceived him. They too were condemned, and all the culprits would have been taken to prison and shut up for the rest of their lives, if those they had injured had not pleaded for their forgiveness. Guna-Vara and her son prostrated themselves at the foot of the throne, and would not rise till they had won pardon for their enemies. Ayasolekha and the brothers were allowed to go free; but Sringa-Bhuja, though he was the youngest of all the princes, was proclaimed heir to the crown after his father's death. His brothers, however, never ceased to hate him; and when he came to the throne, they gave him a great deal of trouble. He had many years of happiness with his wife and parents before that, and never regretted the mistake about the jewelled arrow; since but for it he would, he knew, never have seen his beloved Rupa-Sikha.

STORY VI

THE BEETLE AND THE
SILKEN THREAD²

CHAPTER I

The strange adventures related in the story of the Beetle
and the Silken Thread took place in the town of Allahabad, "the City of God," so called because it is situated
near the point of meeting of the two sacred rivers of India,
the Ganges, which the Hindus lovingly call Mother Ganga
because they believe its waters can wash away their sins, and
the Jumna, which they consider scarcely less holy.

The ruler of Allahabad was a very selfish and hot-tem-
pered Raja named Surya Pratap, signifying "Powerful as the
Sun," who expected everybody to obey him without a moment's delay, and was ready to punish in a very cruel manner those who hesitated to do so. He would never listen to
a word of explanation, or own that he had been mistaken,
even when he knew full well that he was in the wrong. He
had a mantri, that is to say, a chief vizier or officer, whom
he greatly trusted, and really seemed to be fond of, for he
liked to have him always near him. The vizier was called
Dhairya-Sila, or "the Patient One," because he never lost
his temper, no matter what provocation he received. He had
a beautiful house, much money and many jewels, carriages
to drive about in, noble horses to ride and many servants to

2   There are seventy-two versions of this tale in vogue amongst
the high 3castes of India; the one here given is taken from Raj-Yoga, the
highest form of Hindu ascetic philosophy.

wait upon him, all given to him by his master. But what he loved best of all was his faithful wife, Buddhi-Mati, or "the Sensible One," whom he had chosen for himself, and who would have died for him.

Many of the Raja's subjects were jealous of Dhairya-Sila, and constantly brought accusations against him, of none of which his master took any notice, except to punish those who tried to set him against his favourite. It really seemed as if nothing would ever bring harm to Dhairya-Sila; but he often told his wife that such good fortune was not likely to last, and that she must be prepared for a change before long.

It turned out that he was right. For one day Surya Pratap ordered him to do what he considered would be a shameful deed. He refused; telling his master that he was wrong to think of such a thing, and entreating him to give up his purpose. "All your life long," he said, "you will wish you had listened to me; for your conscience will never let you rest!"

On hearing these brave words, Surya Pratap flew into a terrible rage, summoned his guards, and ordered them to take Dhairya-Sila outside the city to a very lofty tower, and leave him at the top of it, without shelter from the sun and with nothing to eat or drink. The guards were at first afraid to touch the vizier, remembering how others had been punished for only speaking against him. Seeing their unwillingness, the Raja got more and more angry; but Dhairya-Sila himself kept quite calm, and said to the soldiers:

"I go with you gladly. It is for the master to command and for me to obey."

CHAPTER II

The guards were relieved to find they need not drag the vizier away; for they admired his courage and felt sure that the Raja would soon find he could not get on without him. It might go hardly with them if he suffered harm at their hands. So they only closed in about him; and holding himself very upright, Dhairya-Sila walked to the tower as if he were quite glad to go. In his heart however he knew full well that it would need all his skill to escape with his life.

When her husband did not come home at night, Buddhi-Mati was very much distressed. She guessed at once that something had gone wrong, and set forth to try and find out what had happened. This was easy enough; for as she crept along, with her veil closely held about her lest she should be recognised, she passed groups of people discussing the terrible fate that had befallen the favourite. She decided that she must wait until midnight, when the streets would be deserted and she could reach the tower unnoticed. It was almost dark when she got there, but in the dim light of the stars she made out the form of him she loved better than herself, leaning over the edge of the railing at the top.

"Is my dear lord still alive?" she whispered, "and is there anything I can do to help him?"

"You can do everything that is needed to help me," answered Dhairya-Sila quietly, "if you only obey every direction I give you. Do not for one moment suppose that I am in despair. I am more powerful even now than my master, who has but shown his weakness by attempting to harm me. Now listen to me. Come to-morrow night at this very hour, bringing with you the following things: first, a beetle; secondly, sixty yards of the finest silk thread, as thin as a spider's web; thirdly, sixty yards of cotton thread, as thin as you can get it, but very strong; fourthly, sixty yards of good stout twine; fifthly, sixty yards of rope, strong enough to carry my weight; and last, but certainly not least, one drop of the purest bees' honey."

CHAPTER III

Buddhi-Mati listened very attentively to these strange instructions, and began to ask questions about them. "Why do you want the beetle? Why do you want the honey?" and so on. But her husband checked her. "I have no strength to waste in explanations," he said. "Go home in peace, sleep well, and dream of me." So the anxious wife went meekly away; and early the next day she set to work to obey the orders she had received. She had some trouble in obtaining fine enough silk, so very, very thin it had to be, like a spider's web; but the cotton, twine and rope were easily bought; and to her surprise she was not asked what she wanted them for. It took her a good while to choose the beetle. For though she had a vague kind of idea that the silk, the cotton, twine, and rope, were to help her husband get down from the tower, she could not imagine what share the beetle and the honey were to take. In the end she chose a very handsome, strong-looking, brilliantly coloured fellow who lived in the garden of her home and whom she knew to be fond of honey.

CHAPTER IV

All the time Buddhi-Mati was at work for her husband, she was thinking of him and looking forward to the happy day of his return home. She had such faith in him that she did not for a moment doubt that he would escape; but she was anxious about the future, feeling sure that the Raja would never forgive Dhairya-Sila for being wiser than himself. Exactly at the time fixed the faithful wife appeared at the foot of the tower, with all the things she had been told to bring with her.

"Is all well with my lord?" she whispered, as she gazed up through the darkness. "I have the silken thread as fine as gossamer, the cotton thread, the twine, the rope, the beetle and the honey."

"Yes," answered Dhairya-Sila, "all is still well with me. I have slept well, feeling confident that my dear one would bring all that is needed for my safety; but I dread the great heat of another day, and we must lose no time in getting away from this terrible tower. Now attend most carefully to all I bid you do; and remember not to speak loud, or the sentries posted within hearing will take alarm and drive you away. First of all, tie the end of the silken thread round the middle of the beetle, leaving all its legs quite free. Then rub the drop of honey on its nose, and put the little creature on the wall, with its nose turned upwards towards me. It will smell the honey, but will not guess that it carries it itself, and it will crawl upwards in the hope of getting to the hive from which that honey came. Keep the rest of the silk firmly held, and gradually unwind it as the beetle climbs up. Mind you do not let it slip, for my very life depends on that slight link with you."

CHAPTER V

Buddhi-Mati, though her hands shook and her heart beat fast as she realized all that depended on her, kept the silk from becoming entangled; and when it was nearly all unwound, she heard her husband's voice saying to her: "Now tie the cotton thread to the end of the silk that you hold, and let it gradually unwind." She obeyed, fully understanding now what all these preparations were for.

When the little messenger of life reached the top of the tower, Dhairya-Sila took it up in his hand and very gently unfastened the silken thread from its body. Then he placed the beetle carefully in a fold of his turban, and began to pull the silken thread up—very, very slowly, for if it had broken, his wonderful scheme would have come to an end. Presently he had the cotton thread in his fingers, and he broke off the silk, wound it up, and placed it too in his turban. It had done its duty well, and he would not throw it away.

"Half the work is done now," he whispered to his faithful wife. "You have all but saved me now. Take the twine and tie it to the end of the cotton thread."

Very happily Buddhi-Mati obeyed once more; and soon the cotton thread and twine were also laid aside, and the strong rope tied to the last was being quickly dragged up by the clever vizier, who knew that all fear of death from sunstroke or hunger was over. When he had all the rope on the tower, he fastened one end of it to the iron railing which ran round the platform on which he stood, and very quickly slid down to the bottom, where his wife was waiting for him, trembling with joy.

CHAPTER VI

After embracing his wife and thanking her for saving him, the vizier said to her: "Before we return home, let us give thanks to the great God who helped me in my need by putting into my head the device by which I escaped." The happy pair then prostrated themselves on the ground, and in fervent words of gratitude expressed their sense of what the God they worshipped had done for them. "And now," said Dhairya-Sila, "the next thing we have to do is to take the dear little beetle which was the instrument of my rescue back to the place it came from." And taking off his turban, he showed his wife the tiny creature lying in the soft folds.

Buddhi-Mati led her husband to the garden where she had found the beetle, and Dhairya-Sila laid it tenderly on the ground, fetched some food for it, such as he knew it loved, and there left it to take up its old way of life. The rest of the day he spent quietly in his own home with his wife, keeping out of sight of his servants, lest they should report his return to his master. "You must never breathe a word to any one of how I escaped," Dhairya-Sila said, and his wife promised that she never would.

CHAPTER VII

All this time the Raja was feeling very unhappy, for he thought he had himself caused the death of the one man he could trust. He was too proud to let anybody know that he missed Dhairya-Sila, and was longing to send for him from the tower before it was too late. What then was his relief and surprise when a message was brought to him that the vizier was at the door of the palace and begged for an interview.

"Bring him in at once," cried Surya Pratap. And the next moment Dhairya-Sila stood before his master, his hands folded on his breast and his head bent in token of his submission. The attendants looked on, eager to know how he had got down from the tower, some of them anything but glad to see him back. The Raja took care not to show how delighted he was to see him, and pretending to be angry, he said:

"How dare you come into my presence, and which of my subjects has ventured to help you to escape the death on the tower you so richly deserved?"

"None of your subjects, great and just and glorious ruler," replied Dhairya-Sila, "but the God who created us both, making you my master and me your humble servant. It was that God," he went on, "who saved me, knowing that I was indeed guiltless of any crime against you. I had not been long on the tower when help came to me in the form of a great and noble eagle, which appeared above me, hovering with outspread wings, as if about to swoop down upon me and tear me limb from limb. I trembled greatly, but I need have had no fear; for instead of harming me, the bird suddenly lifted me up in its talons and, flying rapidly through the air, landed me upon the balcony of my home and disappeared. Great indeed was the joy of my wife at my rescue from what seemed to be certain death; but I tore myself away from her embraces, to come and tell my lord how heaven had interfered to prove my innocence."

Fully believing that a miracle had taken place, Surya Pratap asked no more questions, but at once restored Dhairya-Sila to his old place as vizier, taking care not again to ill-treat the man he now believed to be under the special care of God. Though he certainly did not deserve it, the vizier prospered greatly all the rest of his life and as time went on he became the real ruler of the kingdom, for the Raja depended on his advice in everything. He grew richer and richer, but he was never really happy again, remembering the lie he had told to the master to whom he owed so much. Buddhi-Mati could never understand why he made up the story about the eagle, and constantly urged him to tell the truth. She thought it was really far more wonderful that a little beetle should have been the means of rescuing him, than that a strong bird should have done so; and she wanted everyone to know what a very clever husband she had. She kept her promise never to tell anyone what really happened, but the secret came out for all that. By the time it was known, however, Dhairya-Sila was so powerful that no one could harm him, and when he died his son took his place as vizier,

A CROW AND HIS THREE FRIENDS

CHAPTER I

In the branches of a great tree, in a forest in India, lived a wise old crow in a very comfortable, well-built nest. His wife was dead, and all his children were getting their own living; so he had nothing to do but to look after himself. He led a very easy existence, but took a great interest in the affairs of his neighbours. One day, popping his head over the edge of his home, he saw a fierce-looking man stalking along, carrying a stick in one hand and a net in the other.

"That fellow is up to some mischief, I'll be bound," thought the crow: "I will keep my eye on him." The man stopped under the tree, spread the net on the ground; and taking a bag of rice out of his pocket, he scattered the grains amongst the meshes of the net. Then he hid himself behind the trunk of the tree from which the crow was watching, evidently intending to stop there and see what would happen. The crow felt pretty gore that the stranger had designs against birds, and that the stick had something to do with the matter. He was quite right; and it was not long before just what he expected came to pass.

A flock of pigeons, led by a specially fine bird who had been chosen king because of his size and the beauty of his plumage, came flying rapidly along, and noticed the white rice, but did not see the net, because it was very much the same colour as the ground. Down swooped the king, and down swept all the other pigeons, eager to enjoy a good meal without any trouble to themselves. Alas, their joy was short lived! They were all caught in the net and began struggling to escape, beating the air with their wings and uttering loud cries of distress.

The crow and the man behind the tree kept very quiet, watching them; the man with his stick ready to beat the poor helpless birds to death, the crow watching out of mere curiosity. Now a very strange and wonderful thing came to pass. The king of the pigeons, who had his wits about him, said to the imprisoned birds:

"Take the net up in your beaks, all of you spread out your wings at once, and fly straight up into the air as quickly as possible."

CHAPTER II

In a moment all the pigeons, who were accustomed to obey their leader, did as they were bid; each little bird seized a separate thread of the net in his beak and up, up, up, they all flew, looking very beautiful with the sunlight gleaming on their white wings. Very soon they were out of sight; and the man, who thought he had hit upon a very clever plan, came forth from his hiding-place, very much surprised at what had happened. He stood gazing up after his vanished net for a little time, and then went away muttering to himself, whilst the wise old crow laughed at him.

When the pigeons had flown some distance, and were beginning to get exhausted, for the net was heavy and they were quite unused to carrying loads, the king bade them rest awhile in a clearing of the forest; and as they all lay on the ground panting for breath, with the cruel net still hampering them, he said:

"What we must do now is to take this horrible net to my old friend Hiranya the mouse, who will, I am quite sure, nibble through the strings for me and set us all free. He lives, as you all know, near the tree where the net was spread, deep underground; but there are many passages leading to his home, and we shall easily find one of the openings. Once there, we will all lift up our voices, and call to him at once, when he will be sure to hear us." So the weary pigeons took up their burden once more, and sped back whence they had come, greatly to the surprise of the crow, who wondered at their coming back to the very place where misfortune had overtaken them. He very soon learnt the reason, and got so excited watching what was going on, that he hopped out of his nest and perched upon a branch where he could see better. Presently a great clamour arose, one word being repeated again and again: "Hiranya! Hiranya! Hiranya."

"Why, that's the name of the mouse who lives down below there!" thought the crow. "Now, what good can he do? I know, I know," he added, as he remembered the sharp teeth of Hiranya. "That king of the pigeons is a sensible fellow. I must make friends with him."

Very soon, as the pigeons lay fluttering and struggling outside one of the entrances to Hiranya's retreat, the mouse came out. He didn't even need to be told what was wanted, but at once began to nibble the string, first setting free the king, and then all the rest of the birds. "A friend in need is a friend indeed," cried the king; "a thousand thousand thanks!" And away he flew up into the beautiful free air of heaven, followed by the happy pigeons, none of them ever likely to forget the adventure or to pick up food from the ground without a good look at it first.

CHAPTER III

The mouse did not at once return to his hole when the birds were gone, but went for a little stroll, which brought him to the ground still strewn with rice, which he began to eat with great relish. "It's an ill wind," he said to himself, "which brings nobody any good. There's many a good meal for my whole family here."

Presently he was joined by the old crow, who had flown down from his perch unnoticed by Hiranya, and now addressed him in his croaky voice:

"Hiranya," he said, "for that I know is your name, I am called Laghupatin and I would gladly have you for a friend. I have seen all that you did for the pigeons, and have come to the conclusion that you are a mouse of great wisdom, ready to help those who are in trouble, without any thought of yourself."

"You are quite wrong," squeaked Hiranya. "I am not so silly as you make out. I have no wish to be your friend. If you were hungry, you wouldn't hesitate to gobble me up. I don't care for that sort of affection."

With that Hiranya whisked away to his hole, pausing at the entrance, when he knew the crow could not get at him, to cry, "You be off to your nest and leave me alone!"

The feelings of the crow were very much hurt at this speech, the more that he knew full well it was not exactly love for the mouse, which had led him to make his offer, but self-interest: for who could tell what difficulties he himself might some day be in, out of which the mouse might help him? Instead of obeying Hiranya, and going back to his nest, he hopped to the mouse's hole, and putting his head on one side in what he thought was a very taking manner, he said:

"Pray do not misjudge me so. Never would I harm you! Even if I did not wish to have you for a friend, I should not dream of gobbling you up, as you say, however hungry I might be. Surely you are aware that I am a strict vegetarian, and never eat the flesh of other creatures. At least give me a trial. Let us share a meal together, and talk the matter over."

CHAPTER IV

Hiranya, on hearing the last remark of Laghupatin, hesitated, and in the end he agreed that he would have supper with the crow that very evening. "There is plenty of rice here," he said, "which we can eat on the spot. It would be impossible for you to get into my hole, and I am certainly not disposed to visit you in your nest." So the two at once began their meal, and before it was over they had become good friends. Not a day passed without a meeting, and when all the rice was eaten up, each of the two would bring something to the feast. This had gone on for some little time, when the crow, who was fond of adventure and change, said one day to the mouse: "Don't you think we might go somewhere else for a time? I am rather tired of this bit of the forest, every inch of which we both know well. I've got another great friend who lives beside a fine river a few miles away, a tortoise named Mandharaka; a thoroughly good, trustworthy fellow he is, though rather slow and cautious in his ways. I should like to introduce you to him. There are quantities of food suitable for us both where he lives, for it is a very fruitful land. What do you say to coming with me to pay him a visit?"

"How in the world should I get there?" answered Hiranya. "It's all very well for you, who can fly. I can't walk for miles and miles. For all that I too am sick of this place and would like a change."

"Oh, there's no difficulty about that," replied Laghupatin. "I will carry you in my beak, and you will get there without any fatigue at all." To this Hiranya consented, and very early one morning the two friends started off together.

CHAPTER V

After flying along for several hours, the crow began to feel very tired. He was seized too with a great desire to hear his own voice again. So he flew to the ground, laid his little companion gently down, and gave vent to a number of hoarse cries, which quite frightened Hiranya, who timidly asked him what was the matter.

"Nothing whatever," answered Laghupatin, "except that you are not quite so light as I thought you were, and that I need a rest; besides which, I am hungry and I expect you are. We had better stop here for the night, and start again early to-morrow morning." Hiranya readily agreed to this, and after a good meal, which was easily found, the two settled down to sleep, the crow perched in a tree, the mouse hidden amongst its roots. Very early the next day they were off again, and soon arrived at the river, where they were warmly welcomed by the tortoise. The three had a long talk together, and agreed never to part again. The tortoise, who had lived a great deal longer than either the mouse or the crow, was a very pleasant companion; and even Laghupatin, who was very fond of talking himself, liked to listen to his stories of long ago.

"I wonder," said the tortoise, whose name was Mandharaka, to the mouse, "that you are not afraid to travel about as you have done, with your soft little body unprotected by any armour. Look how different it is for me; it is almost impossible for any of the wild creatures who live near this river to hurt me, and they know it full well. See how thick and strong my armour is. The claws even of a tiger, a wild cat or an eagle, could not penetrate it. I am very much afraid, my little friend, that you will be gobbled up some fine day, and Laghupatin and I will seek for you in vain."

"Of course," said the mouse, "I know the truth of what you say; but I can very easily hide from danger—much more easily than you or Laghupatin. A tuft of moss or a few dead leaves are shelter enough for me, but big fellows like you and the crow can be quite easily seen. Nobody saw me when the pigeons were all caught except Laghupatin; and I would have kept out of his sight if I had not known that he did not care to eat mice."

In spite of the fears of Mandharaka, the mouse and the crow lived as his guests for a long time without any accident; and one day they were suddenly joined by a new companion, a creature as unlike any one of the three friends as could possibly be imagined. This was a very beautiful deer, who came bounding out of the forest, all eager to escape from the hunters, by whom he had been pursued, but too weary to reach the river, across which he had hoped to be able to swim to safety. Just as he reached the three friends, he fell to the ground, almost crushing the mouse, who darted away in the nick of time. Strange to say, the hunters did not follow the deer; and it was evident that they had not noticed the way he had gone.

The tortoise, the crow and the mouse were all very sorry for the deer, and, as was always the case, the crow was the first to speak. "Whatever has happened to you?" he asked. And the deer made answer:

"I thought my last hour had come this time, for the hunters were close upon me; and even now I do not feel safe."

"I'll fly up and take a look 'round," said Laghupatin; and off he went to explore, coming back soon, to say he had seen the hunters disappearing a long distance off, going in quite another direction from the river. Gradually the deer was re-assured, and lay still where he had fallen; whilst the three friends chatted away to him, telling him of their adventures. "What you had better do," said the tortoise, "is to join us. When you have had a good meal, and a drink from the river, you will feel a different creature. My old friend Laghupatin will be the one to keep watch for us all, and warn us of any danger approaching; I will give you the benefit of my long experience; and little Hiranya, though he is not likely to be of any use to you, will certainly never do you any harm."

CHAPTER VI

The deer was so touched by the kind way in which he had been received, that he agreed to stop with the three friends; and for some weeks after his arrival all went well. Each member of the party went his own way during the day-time, but all four met together in the evening, and took it in turns to tell their adventures. The crow always had the most to say, and was very useful to the deer in warning him of the presence of hunters in the forest. One beautiful moonlight night the deer did not come back as usual, and the other three became very anxious about him. The crow flew up to the highest tree near and eagerly sought for some sign of his lost friend, of whom he had grown very fond. Presently he noticed a dark mass by the river-side, just where the deer used to go down to drink every evening. "That must be he," thought the crow; and very soon he was hovering above the deer, who had been caught in a net and was struggling in vain to get free.

The poor deer was very glad indeed to see the crow, and cried to him in a piteous voice: "Be quick, be quick, and help me, before the terrible hunters find me and kill me."

"I can do nothing for you myself," said the crow, "but I know who can. Remember who saved the pigeons!" And away he flew to fetch little Hiranya, who with the tortoise was anxiously awaiting his return. Very soon Laghupatin was back by the river-side with the little mouse in his beak; and it did not take long for Hiranya, who had been despised by the deer and the tortoise as a feeble little thing, to nibble through the cords and save the life of the animal a hundred times as big as himself.

How happy the deer was when the cruel cords were loosed and he could stretch out his limbs again! He bounded up, but took great care not to crush the mouse, who had done him such a service. "Never, never, never," he said, "shall I forget what you have done for me. Ask anything in my power, and I will do it."

"I want nothing," said Hixanya, "except the joyful thought of having saved you."

By this time the tortoise had crept to the river-bank, and he too was glad that the deer had been saved. He praised the mouse, and declared that he would never again look down upon him. Then the four started to go back to their usual haunt in the forest; the deer, the crow, and the mouse soon arriving there quite safely, whilst the tortoise, who could only get along very slowly, lagged behind. Now came the time for him to find out that armour was not the only thing needed to save him from danger. He had not got very far from the riverbank before the cruel hunter who had set the net to catch the deer, came to see if he had succeeded. Great was his rage when he found the net lying on the ground, but not exactly where he had left it. He guessed at once that some animal had been caught in it and escaped after a long struggle. He looked carefully about and noticed that the cords had been bitten through here and there. So he suspected just what had happened, and began to search about for any creature who could have done the mischief.

There was not a sign of the mouse, but the slow-moving tortoise was soon discovered, and pouncing down upon him, the hunter rolled him up in another net he had with him, and carried him off, "It's not much of a prize," said the hunter to himself, "but better than nothing. I'll have my revenge on the wretched creature anyhow, as I have lost the prey I sought."

CHAPTER VII

When the tortoise in his turn did not come home, the deer, the crow and the mouse were very much concerned. They talked the matter over together and decided that, however great the risk to themselves, they must go back and see what had become of their friend. This time the mouse travelled in one of the eats of the deer, from which he peeped forth with his bright eyes, hoping to see the tortoise toiling along in his usual solemn manner; whilst the crow, also on the watch, flew along beside them. Great was the surprise and terror of all three when, as they came out of the forest, they saw the hunter striding along towards them, with the tortoise in the net under his arm. Once more the little mouse showed his wisdom. Without a moment's hesitation he said to the deer: "Throw yourself on the ground and pretend to be dead; and you," he added to the crow, "perch on his head and bend over as if you were going to peck out his eyes."

Without any idea what Hiranya meant by these strange orders, but remembering how he had helped in other dangers, the two did as they were told; the poor deer feeling anything but happy lying still where his enemy was sure to see him, and thereby proving what a noble creature he was. The hunter did, see him very soon, and thinking to himself, "After all I shall get that deer," he let the tortoise fall, and came striding along as fast as he could.

Up jumped the deer without waiting to see what became of the tortoise, and sped away like the wind. The hunter rushed after him, and the two were soon out of sight. The tortoise, whose armour had saved him from being hurt by his fall, was indeed pleased when he saw little Hiranya running towards him. "Be quick, be quick!" he cried, "and set me free." Very soon the sharp teeth of the mouse had bitten through the meshes of the net, and before the hunter came back, after trying in vain to catch the deer, the tortoise was safely swimming across the river, leaving the net upon the ground, whilst the crow and the mouse were back in the shelter of the forest.

"There's some magic at work here," said the hunter when, expecting to find the tortoise where he had left him, he discovered that his prisoner had escaped. "The stupid beast could not have got out alone," he added, as he picked up the net and walked off with it. "But he wasn't worth keeping anyhow."

That evening the four friends met once more, and talked over all they had gone through together. The deer and the tortoise were full of gratitude to the mouse, and could not say enough in his praise, but the crow was rather sulky, and remarked: "If it had not been for me, neither of you would ever have seen Hiranya. He was my friend before he was yours."

"You are right," said the tortoise, "and you must also remember that it was my armour which saved me from being killed in that terrible fall."

"Your armour would not have been of much use to you, if the hunter had been allowed to carry you to his home," said the deer. "In my opinion you and I both owe our lives entirely to Hiranya. He is small and weak, it is true, but he has better brains than any of the rest of us, and I for one admire him with all my heart. I am glad I trusted him and obeyed him, when he ordered me to pretend to be dead, for I had not the least idea how that could help the tortoise."

"Have it your own way," croaked the crow, "but I keep my own opinion all the same. But for me you would never have known my dear little Hiranya."

In spite of this little dispute the four friends were soon as happy together as before the adventure of the tortoise. They once more agreed never to part and lived happily together for many years, as they had done ever since they first met.

STORY VIII

A CLEVER THIEF

CHAPTER I

A certain man, named Hari-Sarman, who lived in a little village in India, where there were no rich people and everyone had to work hard to get his daily bread, got very weary of the life he had to lead. He had a wife whose name was Vidya, and a large family; and even if he had been very industrious it would have been difficult for him to get enough food for them all. Unfortunately he was not a bit industrious, but very lazy, and so was his wife. Neither of them made any attempt to teach their boys and girls to earn their own living; and if the other poor people in the village had not helped them, they would have starved. Hari-Sarman used to send his children out in different directions to beg or steal, whilst he and Vidya stayed at home doing nothing.

One day he said to his wife: "Let us leave this stupid place, and go to some big city where we can pick up a living of some kind. I will pretend to be a wise man, able to find out secrets; and you can say that you know all about children, having had so many of your own." Vidya gladly agreed to this, and the whole party set out, carrying the few possessions they had with them. In course of time they came to a big town, and Hari-Sarman went boldly to the chief house in it, leaving his wife and children outside. He asked to see the master, and was taken into his presence. This master was a very rich merchant, owning large estates in the country; but he cannot have been very clever, for he was at once quite taken in by the story Hari-Sarman told him. He said that he would find work for him and his wife, and that the children could be sent to a farm he had, in the country, where they could be made very useful.

Overjoyed at this, Hari-Sarman hastened out to tell his wife the good news; and the two were at once received into the grand residence, in which a small room was given to them for their own, whilst the children were taken away to the farm, fall of eager delight at the change from the wretched life they had been leading.

CHAPTER II

Soon after the arrival of the husband and wife at the merchant's house, a very important event took place, namely, the marriage of the eldest daughter. Great were the preparations beforehand, in which Vidya took her full share, helping in the kitchen to make all manner of delicious dishes, and living in great luxury herself. For there was no stint in the wealthy home; even the humblest servants were well cared for. Vidya was happier than she had ever been before, now that she had plenty to do and plenty of good food. She became in fact quite a different creature, and began to wish she had been a better mother to her children. "When the wedding is over," she thought, "I will go and see how they are getting on." On the other hand she forgot all about her husband and scarcely ever saw him.

It was all very different with Hari-Sarman himself. He had no special duties to perform and nobody seemed to want him. If he went into the kitchen, the busy servants ordered him to get out of their way; and he was not made welcome by the owner of the house or his guests. The merchant too forgot all about him, and he felt very lonely and miserable. He had been thinking to himself how much he would enjoy all the delicious food he would get after the wedding; and now he began to grumble: "I'm starving in the midst of plenty, that's what I am. Something will have to be done to change this horrible state of things."

Whilst the preparations for the wedding were going on, Vidya never came near her husband, and he lay awake a long time thinking, "What in the world can I do to make the master send for me?" All of a sudden an idea came into his head. "I'll steal something valuable, and hide it away; and when everyone is being asked about the loss, the merchant will remember the man who can reveal secrets. Now what can I take that is sure to be missed? I know, I know!" And springing out of bed, he hastily dressed himself and crept out of the house.

CHAPTER III

This was what Hari-Sarman decided to do. The merchant had a great many very beautiful horses, which lived in splendid stables and were taken the greatest possible care of. Amongst them was a lovely little Arab mare, the special favourite of the bride, who often went to pet it and give it sugar. "I'll steal that mare and hide it away in the forest," said the wicked man to himself. "Then, when every one is hunting for her, the master will remember the man who can reveal secrets and send for me. Ah! Ah! What a clever fellow I am! Ah the stablemen and grooms are feasting, I know; for I saw them myself when I tried to get hold of my wife. I can climb through a window that is always left open." It turned out that he was right. He met no one on his way to the stables, which ware quite deserted. He got in easily, opened, the door from inside, and led out the little mare, which made no resistance; she had always been so kindly treated that she was not a bit afraid. He took the beautiful creature far into the depths of the forest, tied her up there, and got safely back to his own room without being seen.

Early the next morning the merchant's daughter, attended by her maidens, went to see her dear little mare, taking with her an extra supply of sugar. What was her distress when she found the stall empty! She guessed at once that a thief had got in during the night, and hurried home to tell her father, who was very, very angry with the stablemen who had deserted their posts, and declared they should all be flogged for it. "But the first thing to do is to get the mare back," he said; and he ordered messengers to be sent in every direction, promising a big reward to anyone who brought news of the mare.

Vidya of course heard all there was to hear, and at once suspected that Hari-Sarman had had something to do with the matter. "I expect he has hidden the mare," she thought to herself, "and means to get the reward for finding it." So she asked to see the master of the house, and when leave was granted to her she said to him:

"Why do you not send for my husband, the man who can reveal secrets, because of the wonderful power that has been given him of seeing what is hidden from others? Many a time has he surprised me by what he has been able to do."

CHAPTER IV

On hearing what Vidya said, the merchant at once told her to go and fetch her husband. But to her surprise Hari-Sarman refused to go back with her. "You can tell the master what you like," he said, angrily. "You all forgot me entirely yesterday; and now you want me to help you, you suddenly remember my existence. I am not going to be at your beck and call or anyone else's."

Vidya entreated him to listen to reason, but it was no good. She had to go back and tell the merchant that he would not come. Instead of being made angry by this, however, the master surprised her by saying: "Your husband is right. I have treated him badly. Go and tell him I apologise, and will reward him well, if only he will come and help me."

Back again went Vidya and this time she was more successful. But though Hari-Sarman said he would go back with her, he was very sulky and would not answer any of her questions. She could not understand him, and wished she had not left him to himself for so long. He behaved very strangely too when the master, who received him very kindly, asked him if he could tell him where the mare was. "I know," he said, "what a wise and clever man you are."

"It didn't seem much like it yesterday," grumbled Hari-Sarman. "Nobody took any notice of me then, but now you want something of me, you find out that I am wise and clever. I am just the same person, that I was yesterday."

"I know, I know," said the merchant, "and I apologise for my neglect; but when a man's daughter is going to be married, it's no wonder some one gets neglected."

CHAPTER V

Hari-Sarman now thought it was time to take a different tone. So he put his hand in his pocket, and brought out a map he had got ready whilst waiting to be sent for, as he had felt sure he would be. He spread it out before the merchant, and pointed to a dark spot in the midst of many lines crossing each other in a bewildering manner, which he explained were pathways through the forest. "Under a tree, where that dark spot is, you will find the mare," he said.

Overjoyed at the good news, the merchant at once sent a trusted servant to test the truth; and when the mare was brought back, nothing seemed too good for the man who had led to her recovery. At the wedding festivities Hari-Sarman was treated as an honoured guest, and no longer had he any need to complain of not having food enough. His wife of course thought he would forgive her now for having neglected him. But not a bit of it: he still sulked with her, and she could never feel quite sure what the truth was about the mare.

All went well with Hari-Sarman for a long time. But presently something happened which seemed likely to get him into very great trouble. A quantity of gold and many valuable jewels disappeared in the palace of the king of the country; and when the thief could not be discovered, some one told the king the story of the stolen mare, and how a man called Hari-Sarman, living in the house of a rich merchant in the chief city, had found her when everyone else had failed.

"Fetch that man here at once," ordered the king, and very soon Hari-Sarman was brought before him. "I hear you are so wise, you can reveal all secrets," said the king. "Now tell me immediately who has stolen the gold and jewels and where they are to be found."

Poor Hari-Sarman did not know what to say or do. "Give me till to-morrow," he replied in a faltering voice; "I must have a little time to think."

"I will not give you a single hour," answered the king. For seeing the man before him was frightened, he began to suspect he was a deceiver. "If you do not at once tell me where the gold and jewels are, I will have you flogged until you find your tongue."

Hearing this, Hari-Sarman, though more terrified than ever, saw that his only chance of gaining time to make up some story was to get the king to believe in him. So he drew himself up and answered: "The wisest magicians need to employ means to find out the truth. Give me twenty-four hours, and I will name the thieves."

"You are not much of a magician if you cannot find out such a simple thing as I ask of you," said the king. And turning to the guards, he ordered them to take Hari-Sarman to prison, and shut him up there without food or drink till he came to his senses. The man was dragged away, and very soon he found himself alone in a dark and gloomy room from which he saw no hope of escape.

He was in despair and walked up and down, trying in vain to think of some way of escape. "I shall die here of starvation, unless my wife finds some means of setting me free," he said. "I wish I had treated her better instead of being so sulky with her." He tried the bars of the window, but they were very strong: he could not hope to move them. And he beat against the door, but no notice was taken of that.

CHAPTER VI

When it got quite dark in the prison, Hari-Sarman began to talk to himself aloud. "Oh," he said, "I wish I had bitten my tongue out before I told that lie about the mare. It is all my foolish tongue which has got me into this trouble. Tongue! Tongue!" he went on, "it is all your fault."

Now a very strange thing happened. The money and jewels had been stolen by a man, who had been told where they were by a young servant girl in the palace whose name was Jihva, which is the Sanskrit word for tongue; and this girl was in a great fright when she heard that a revealer of secrets had been taken before the king. "He will tell of my share in the matter," she thought, "and I shall get into trouble," It so happened that the guard at the prison door was fond of her, as well as the thief who had stolen the money and jewels. So when all was quiet in the palace, Jihva slipped away to see if she could get that guard to let her see the prisoner. "If I promise to give him part of the money," she thought, "he will undertake not to betray me."

The guard was glad enough when Jihva came to talk to him, and he let her listen at the key-hole to what Hari-Sarman was saying. Just imagine her astonishment when she heard him repeating her name again and again. "Jihva! Jihva! Thou," he cried, "art the cause of this suffering. Why didst thou behave in such a foolish manner, just for the sake of the good things of this life? Never can I forgive thee, Jihva, thou wicked, wicked one!"

"Oh! oh!" cried Jihva in an agony of terror, "he knows the truth; he knows that I helped the thief." And she entreated the guard to let her into the prison that she might plead with Hari-Sarman. not to tell the king what she had done. The man hesitated at first, but in the end she persuaded him to consent by promising him a large reward.

When the key grated in the lock, Hari-Sarman stopped talking aloud, wondering whether what he had been saying had been overheard by the guard, and half hoping that his wife had got leave to come and see him. As the door opened and he saw a woman coming in by the light of a lantern held up by the guard, he cried, "Vidya my beloved!" But he soon realized that it was a stranger. He was indeed surprised and relieved, when Jihva suddenly threw herself at his feet and, clinging to his knees, began to weep and moan "Oh, most holy man," she cried between her sobs, "who knowest the very secrets of the heart, I have come to confess that it was indeed I, Jihva, your humble servant, who aided the thief to take the jewels and the gold and to hide them beneath the big pomegranate tree behind the palace."

"Rise," replied Hari-Sarman, overjoyed at hearing this. "You have told me nothing that I did not know, for no secret is hidden from me. What reward will you give me if I save you from the wrath of the king?"

"I will give you all the money I have," said Jihva; "and that is not a little."

"That also I knew," said Hari-Sarman. "For you have good wages, and many a time you have stolen money that did not belong to you. Go now and fetch it all, and have no fear that I will betray you."

CHAPTER VII

Without waiting a moment Jihva hurried away to fetch the money; but when she got back with it, the man on guard, who had heard everything that had passed between her and Hari-Sarman, would not let her in to the prison again till she gave him ten gold pieces. Thinking that Hari-Sarman really knew exactly how much money she had, Jihva was afraid he would be angry when he missed some of it; and again she let out the truth, which he might never have guessed. For she began at once to say, "I brought all I had, but the man at the door has taken ten pieces." This did vex Hari-Sarman very much, and he told her he would let the king know what she had done, unless she fetched the thief who had taken the money and jewels. "I cannot do that," said Jihva, "for he is very far away. He lives with his brother, Indra Datta, in the forest beyond the river, more than a day's journey from here." "I did but try you," said the clever Hari-Sarman, who now knew who the thief was; "for I can see him where he is at this moment. Now go home and wait there till I send for you."

But Jihva, who loved the thief and did not want him to be punished, refused to go until Hari-Sarman promised that he would not tell the king who the man was or where he lived. "I would rather," she said, "bear all the punishment than that he should suffer." Even Hari-Sarman was touched at this, and fearing that if he kept Jihva longer, she would be found in the prison by messengers from the king, he promised that no harm should come to her or the thief, and let her go.

Very soon after this, messengers came to take Hari-Sarman once more before the king; who received him very coldly and began at once to threaten him with a terrible punishment, if he did not say who the thief was, and where the gold and jewels were. Even now Hari-Sarman pretended to be unwilling to speak. But when he saw that the king would put up with no more delay, he said, "I will lead you to the spot where the treasure is buried, but the name of the thief, though I know it, I will never betray." The king, who did not really care much who the thief was, so long as he got back his money, lost not a moment, but ordered his attendants to get spades and follow him. Very soon Hari-Sarman brought them to the pomegranate tree. And there, sure enough, deep down in the ground, was all that had been lost.

Nothing was now too good for Hari-Sarman: the king was greatly delighted, and heaped riches and honours upon him. But some of the wise men at the court suspected that he was really a deceiver, and set about trying to find out all they could about him. They sent for the man who had been on guard at the prison, and asked him many questions. He did not dare tell the truth, for he knew he would be terribly punished if he let out that Jihva had been allowed to see his prisoner; but he hesitated so much that the wise men knew he was not speaking the truth. One of them, whom the king loved, and trusted very much, whose name was Deva-Jnanin, said to his master: "I do not like to see that man, about whom we really know nothing, treated as he is. He might easily have found out where the treasure was hidden without any special power. Will you not test him in some other way in my presence and that of your chief advisers?"

The king, who was always ready to listen to reason, agreed to this; and after a long consultation with Deva-Jnanin, he decided on a very clever puzzle with which to try Hari-Sarman. A live frog was put into a pitcher; the lid was shut down, and the man who pretended to know everything was brought into the great reception room, where all the wise men of the court were gathered together round the throne, on which sat the king in his royal robes. Deva-Jnanin had been chosen by his master to speak for him; and coming forward, he pointed to the small pitcher on the ground, and said: "Great as are the honours already bestowed on you, they shall be increased if you can say at once what is in that pitcher."

CHAPTER VIII

Hari-Sarman thought whan he looked at the pitcher: "Alas, alas, it is all over with me now! Never can I find out what is in it. Would that I had left this town with the money I had from Jihva before it was too late!" Then he began to mutter to himself, as it was always his habit to do when he was in trouble. It so happened that, when he was a little boy, his father used to call him frog, and now his thoughts went back to the time when he was a happy innocent child, and he said aloud: "Oh, frog, what trouble has come to you! That pitcher will be the death of you!"

Even Deva-Jnanin was astonished when he heard that; and so were all the other wise men. The king was delighted to find that after all he had made no mistake; and all the people who had been allowed to come in to see the trial were greatly excited. Shouting for joy the king called Hari-Sarman to come to the foot of the throne, and told him he would never, never doubt him again. He should have yet more money, a beautiful house in the country as well as the one he already had in the town, and his children should be brought from the farm to live with him and their mother, who should have lovely dresses and ornaments to wear.

Nobody was more surprised than Hari-Sarman himself. He guessed, of course, that there was a frog in the pitcher. And when the king had ended his speech, he said: "One thing I ask in addition to all that has been given me, that I may keep the pitcher in memory of this day, when my truth has been proved once more beyond a doubt."

His request was, of course, granted; and he went off with the pitcher under his arm, full of rejoicing over his narrow escape. At the same time he was also full of fear for the future. He knew only too well that it had only been by a lucky chance that he had used the word Jihva in his first danger and Frog in the second. He was not likely to get off a third time; and he made up his mind that he would skip away some dark night soon, with all the money and jewels he could carry, and be seen no more where such strange adventures had befallen him. He did not even tell his wife what he meant to do, but pretended to have forgiven her entirely for the way she had neglected him when he was poor, and to be glad that their children were to be restored to them. Before they came from the farm their father had disappeared, and nobody ever found out what had become of him; but the king let his family keep what had been given to him, and to the end believed he really had been what he had pretended to be. Only Deva-Jnanin had his doubts; but he kept them to himself, for he thought, "Now the man is gone, it really does not matter who or what he was."

STORY IX

THE HERMIT'S DAUGHTER

CHAPTER I

Near a town in India called Ikshumati, on a beautiful wide river, with trees belonging to a great forest near its banks, there dwelt a holy man named Mana Kanaka, who spent a great part of his life praying to God. He had lost his wife when his only child, a lovely girl called Kadali-Garbha, was only a few months old. Kadali-Garbha was a very happy girl, with many friends in the woods round her home, not children like herself, but wild creatures, who knew she would not do them any harm. They loved her and she loved them. The birds were so tame that they would eat out of her hand, and the deer used to follow her about in the hope of getting the bread she carried in her pocket for them. Her father taught her all she knew, and that was a great deal; for she could read quite learned books in the ancient language of her native land. Better even than what she found out in those books was what Mana Kanaka told her about the loving God of all gods who rules the world and all that live in it. Kadali-Garbha also learnt a great deal through her friendship with wild animals. She knew where the birds built their nests, where the baby deer were born, where the squirrels hid their nuts, and what food all the dwellers in the forest liked best. She helped her father to work in their garden in which all their own food was grown; and she loved to cook the fruit and vegetables for Mana

Kanaka and herself. Her clothes were made of the bark of the trees in the forest, which she herself wove into thin soft material suitable for wearing in a hot climate.

CHAPTER II

Kadali-Garbha never even thought about other children, because she had not been used to having them with her. She was just as happy as the day was long, and never wished for any change. But when she was about sixteen something happened which quite altered her whole life. One day her father had gone into the forest to cut wood, and had left her alone. She had finished tidying the house, and got everything ready for the midday meal, and was sitting at the door of her home, reading to herself, with birds fluttering about her head and a pet doe lying beside her, when she heard the noise of a horse's feet approaching. She looked up, and there on the other side of the fence was a very handsome young man seated on a great black horse, which he had reined up when he caught sight of her. He looked at her without speaking, and she looked back at him with her big black eyes full of surprise at his sudden appearance. She made a beautiful picture, with the green creepers covering the hut behind her, and the doe, which had started up in fear of the horse, pressing against her.

The man was the king of the country, whose name was Dridha-Varman. He had been hunting and had got separated from his attendants. He was very much surprised to find anyone living in the very depths of the forest, and was going to ask the young girl who she was, when Kadali-Garbha saw her father coming along the path leading to his home. Jumping up, she ran to meet him, glad that he had come; for she had never before seen a young man and was as shy as any of the wild creatures of the woods. Now that Mana Kanaka was with her, she got over her fright, and felt quite safe, clinging to his arm as he and the king talked together.

CHAPTER III

Mana Kanaka knew at once that the man on the horse was the king; and a great fear entered his heart when he saw how Dridha-Varman looked at his beloved only child.

"Who are you, and who is that lovely girl?" asked the king. And Mana Kanaka answered, "I am only a humble woodcutter; and this is my only child, whose mother has long been dead."

"Her mother must have been a very lovely woman, if her daughter is like her," said the king. "Never before have I seen such perfect beauty."

"Her mother," replied Mana Kanaka, "was indeed what you say; and her soul was as beautiful as the body in which it dwelt all too short a time."

"I would have your daughter for my wife," said the king; "and if you will give her to me, she shall have no wish ungratified. She shall have servants to wait on her and other young girls to be her companions; beautiful clothes to wear, the best of food to eat, horses and carriages as many as she will, and no work to do with her own hands."

CHAPTER IV

What Kadali-Garbha did was to cling closely to her father, hiding her face on his arm and whispering, "I will not leave you: do not send me away from you, dear father."

Mana Kanaka stroked her hair, and said in a gentle voice:

"But, dear child, your father is old, and must leave you soon. It is a great honour for his little girl to be chosen by the king for his bride. Do not be afraid, but look at him and see how handsome he is and how kind he looks."

Then Kadali-Garbha looked at the king, who smiled at her and looked so charming that her fear began to leave her. She still clung to her father, but no longer hid her face; and

Mana Kanaka begged Kadali-Garbha to let him send her away, so that he might talk with the king alone about the wish he had expressed to marry her. The king consented to this, and Kadali-Garbha gladly ran away. But when she reached the door of her home, she looked back, and knew in her heart that she already loved the king and did not want him to go away.

It did not take long for the matter of the marriage to be settled. For Mana Kanaka, sad though he was to lose his dear only child, was glad that she should be a queen, and have some one to take care of her when he was gone. After this first visit to the little house in the forest the king came every day to see Kadali-Garbha, bringing all kinds of presents for her. She learnt to love him so much that she became as eager as he was for the wedding to be soon. When the day was fixed, the king sent several ladies of his court to dress the bride in clothes more beautiful that she had ever dreamt of; and in them she looked more lovely even than the first day her lover had seen her.

Now amongst these ladies was a very wise woman who could see what was going to happen; and she knew that there would be troubles for the young queen in the palace, because many would be jealous of her happiness. She was very much taken with the beautiful innocent girl, and wanted to help her so much that she managed to get her alone for a few minutes, when she said to her: "I want you to promise me something. It is to take this packet of mustard seeds, hide it in the bosom of your dress, and when you ride to the palace with your husband, strew the seed along the path as you go. You know how quickly mustard grows. Well, it will spring up soon; and if you want to come home again, you can easily find the way by following the green shoots. Alas, I fear they will not have time to wither before you need their help!"

Kadali-Garbha laughed when the wise woman talked about trouble coming to her. She was so happy, she could not believe she would want to come home again so soon.

"My father can come to me when I want him," she said. "I need only tell my dear husband to send for him." But for all that she took the packet of seeds and hid it in her dress.

CHAPTER V

After the wedding was over, the king mounted his beautiful horse, and bending down, took his young wife up before him. Holding her close to him with his right arm, he held the reins in his left hand; and away they went, soon leaving all the attendants far behind them, the queen scattering the mustard seed as she had promised to do. When they arrived at the palace there were great rejoicings, and everybody seemed charmed with the queen, who was full of eager interest in all that she saw.

For several weeks there was nobody in the wide world so happy and light-hearted as the bride. The king spent many hours a day with her, and was never tired of listening to all she had to tell him about her life in the forest with her father. Every day he gave her some fresh proof of his love, and he never refused to do anything she asked him to do. But presently a change came. Amongst the ladies of the court there was a beautiful woman, who had hoped to be queen herself, and hated Kadali-Garbha so much that she made up her mind to get her into disgrace with the king. She asked first one powerful person and then another to help her; but everybody loved the queen, and the wicked woman began to be afraid that those she had told about her wish to harm her would warn the king. So she sought about for some one who did not know Kadali-Garbha, and suddenly remembered a wise woman named Asoka-Mala, who lived in a cave not far from the town, to whom many people used to go for advice in their difficulties. She went to this woman one night, and told her a long story in which there was not one word of truth. The young queen, she said, did not really love the king; and with the help of her father, who was a magician, she meant to poison him. How could this terrible thing be prevented, she asked; and she promised that if only Asoka-Mala would help to save Dridha-Varman, she would give her a great deal of money.

Asoka-Mala guessed at once that the story was not true, and that it was only because the woman was jealous of the beautiful young queen that she wished to hurt her. But she loved money very much. Instead therefore of at once refusing to have anything to do with the matter, she said: "Bring me fifty gold pieces now, and promise me another fifty when the queen is sent away from the palace, and I will tell you what to do."

The wicked woman promised all this at once. The very next night she brought the first fifty pieces of gold to the cave, and Asoka-Mala told her that she must get the barber, who saw the king alone every day, to tell him he had found out a secret about the queen. "You must tell the barber all you have already told me. But be very careful to give some proof of your story. For if you do not do so, you will only have wasted the fifty gold pieces you have already given to me; and, more than that, you will be terribly punished for trying to hurt the queen, whom everybody loves."

CHAPTER VI

The wicked woman went back to the palace, thinking all the way to herself, "How can I get a proof of what is not true?" At last an idea came into her head. She knew that the queen loved to wander in the forest, and that she was not afraid of the wild creatures, but seemed to understand their language. She would tell the barber that Kadali-Garbha was a witch and knew the secrets of the woods; that she had been seen gathering wild herbs, some of them poisonous, and had been heard muttering strange words to herself as she did so.

Early the next morning the cruel woman went to see the barber, and promised him a reward if he would tell the king what she had found out about his wife. "He won't believe you at first," she said; "but you must go on telling him till he does. You are clever, enough," she added, "to make up something he will believe if what I have thought of is no good."

The barber, who had served the king for many years, would not at first agree to help to make him unhappy. But he too liked money very much, and in the end he promised to see what he could do if he was well paid for it. He was, as the wicked woman had said, clever enough; and he knew from long experience just how to talk to his master. He began by asking the king if he had heard of the lovely woman who was sometimes seen by the woodmen wandering about alone in the forest, with wild creatures following her. Remembering how he had first seen Kadali-Garbha, Dridha-Varman at once guessed that she was the lovely woman. But he did not tell the barber so; for he was so proud of his dear wife's beauty that he liked to hear her praised, and wanted the man to go on talking about her. He just said: "What is she like? Is she tall or short, fair or dark?" The barber answered the questions readily. Then he went on to say that it was easy to see that the lady was as clever as she was beautiful; for she knew not only all about animals but also about plants. "Every day," he said, "she gathers quantities of herbs, and I have been told she makes healing medicines of them. Some even go so far as to say she also makes poisons. But, for my part, I do not believe that; she is too beautiful to be wicked."

The king listened, and a tiny little doubt crept into his mind about his wife. She had never told him about the herbs she gathered, although she often chattered about her friends in the forest. Perhaps after all it was not Kadali-Garbha the barber was talking about. He would ask her if she knew anything about making medicines from herbs. He did so when they were alone together, and she said at once, "Oh, yes! My father taught me. But I have never made any since I was married."

"Are you sure?" asked the king; and she answered laughing, "Of course, I am: how could I be anything but sure? I have no need to think of medicine-making, now I am the queen."

Dridha-Varman said no more at the time. But he was troubled; and when the barber came again, he began at once to ask about the woman who had been seen in the woods. The wicked man was delighted, and made up a long story. He said one of the waiting women had told him of what she had seen. The woman, he said, had followed the lady home one day, and that home was not far from the palace. She had seen her bending over a fire above which hung a great saucepan full of water, into which she flung some of the herbs she had gathered, singing as she did so, in a strange language.

"Could it possibly be," thought the king, "that Kadali-Garbha had deceived him? Was she perhaps a witch after all?" He remembered that he really did not know who she was, or who her father was. He had loved her directly he saw her, just because she was so beautiful. What was he to do now? He was quite sure, from the description the barber had given of the woman in the forest, that she was his wife. He would watch her himself in future, and say nothing to her that would make her think he was doing so.

CHAPTER VII

Although the king said nothing to his wife about what the barber had told him, he could not treat her exactly as he did before he heard it, and she very soon began to wonder what she had done to vex him. The first thing she noticed was that one of the ladies of the court always followed her when she went into the forest. She did not like this; because she so dearly loved to be alone with the wild creatures, and they did not come to her when any one else was near. She told the lady to go away, and she pretended to do so; but she only kept a little further off. And though the queen could no longer see her, she knew she was there, and so did the birds and the deer. This went on for a little time; and then Kadali-Garbha asked her husband to tell every one that she was not to be disturbed when she went to see her friends in the forest.

"I am afraid," said the king, "that some harm will come to you. There are wild beasts in the depths of the wood who might hurt you. And what should I do if any harm came to my dear one?"

Kadali-Garbha was grieved when Dridha-Varman said this, for she knew it was not true; and she looked at him so sadly that he felt ashamed of having doubted her. All would perhaps have been well even now, if he had told her of the story he had heard about her, because then she could have proved that it was not true. But he did not do that; he only said, "I cannot let you be alone so far from home. Why not be content with the lovely gardens all round the palace? If you still wish to go to the woods, I will send one of the game-keepers with you instead of the lady who has been watching you. Then he can protect you if any harmful creature should approach."

"If my lord does not wish me to be alone in the forest," answered the queen, "I will be content with the gardens. For no birds or animals would come near me if one of their enemies were with me. But," she added, as her eyes filled with tears, "will not my lord tell me why he no longer trusts his wife, who loves him with all her heart?"

The king was very much touched by what Kadali-Garbha said, but still could not make up his mind to tell her the truth. So he only embraced her fondly, and said she was a good little wife to be so ready to obey him. The queen went away very sadly, wondering to herself what she could do to prove to her dear lord that she loved him as much as ever. She took care never to go outside the palace gardens, but she longed very much for her old freedom, and began to grow pale and thin.

The wicked woman who had tried to do her harm was very much disappointed that she had only succeeded in making her unhappy; so she went again to Asoka-Mala, and promised her more money if only she would think of some plan to get the king to send his wife away. The wise woman considered a long time, and then she said: "You must use the barber again. He goes from house to house, and he must tell the king that the beautiful woman, who used to roam about in the forest collecting herbs, has been seen there again in the dead of the night, when she could be sure no one would find out what she was doing."

Now it so happened that Kadali-Garbha was often unable to sleep because of her grief that the king did not love her so much as he used to do. One night she got so tired of lying awake that she got up very quietly, so as not to disturb her husband, and putting on her sari, she went out into the gardens, hoping that the fresh air might help her to sleep. Presently the king too woke up, and finding that his wife was no longer beside him, he became very uneasy, and was about to go and seek her, when she came back. He asked her where she had been; and she told him exactly what had happened, but she did not explain why she could not sleep.

CHAPTER VIII

When the barber was shaving the king the next morning, he told him he had heard that people were saying the beautiful woman had been seen again one night, gathering herbs and muttering to herself. "They talk, my lord," said the man, "of your own name having been on her lips; and those who love and honour you are anxious for your safety. Maybe the woman is indeed a witch, who for some reason of her own will try to poison you."

Now Dridha-Varman remembered that Kadali-Garbha had left him the night before, "and perhaps," he thought, "at other times when I was asleep." He could scarcely wait until the barber had finished shaving him, so eager was he to find out the truth. He hurried to his wife's private room, but she was not there; and her ladies told him she had not been seen by them that day. This troubled him terribly, and he roused the whole palace to seek her. Messengers were soon hurrying to and fro, but not a trace of her could be found. Dridha-Varman was now quite sure that the woman the barber had talked about was Kadali-Garbha, the wife he had so loved and trusted. "Perhaps," he thought, "she has left poison in my food, and has gone away so as not to see me die." He would neither eat nor drink, and he ordered all the ladies whose duty it was to wait on the queen to be locked up till she was found. Amongst them was the wicked woman who had done all the mischief because of her jealousy of the beautiful young queen, and very much she wished she had never tried to harm her.

CHAPTER IX

In her trouble about the loss of the king's love Kadali-Garbha longed for her father, for she felt sure he would be able to help her. So she determined to go to him. With the aid of the wise woman who had given her the packet of mustard seed, and who had been her best friend at court, she disguised herself as a messenger, and, mounted on a strong little pony, she sped along the path marked out by the young shoots of mustard, reaching her old home in the forest before the night fell. Great indeed was the joy of Mana Kanaka at the sight of his beloved child, and very soon she had poured out all her sorrow to him. The hermit was at first very much enraged with his son-in-law for the way in which he had treated Kadali-Garbha, and declared that he would use all the powers he had to punish him. "Never," he said, "shall he see your dear face again; but I will go to him and call down on him all manner of misfortunes. You know not, dear child, I have never wished you to know, that I am a magician and can make the very beasts of the field and the winds of heaven obey me. I know full well who has made this mischief between you and your husband, and I will see that punishment overtakes them."

"No, no, father," cried Kadali-Garbha; "I will not have any harm done to my dear one, for I love him with all my heart. All I ask of you is to prove to him that I am innocent of whatever fault he thinks I have committed, and to make him love and trust me again."

It was hard work to persuade Mana Kanaka to promise not to harm the king, but in the end he yielded. Together the father and daughter rode back to the palace, and together they were brought before Dridha-Varman, who, in spite of the anger he had felt against his wife, was overjoyed to see her. When he looked at her clinging to Mana Kanaka's arm, as she had done the first time they met, all his old love returned, and he would have taken her in his arms and told her so before the whole court, if she had not drawn back. It was Mana Kanaka who was the first to speak. Drawing himself up to his full height, and pointing to the king, he charged him with having broken his vow to love and protect his wife. "You have listened to lying tongues," he said, "and I will tell you to whom those tongues belong, that justice may be done to them."

Once more Kadali-Garbha interfered. "No, father," she said; "let their names be forgotten: only prove to my lord that I am his loving faithful wife, and I will be content."

"I need no proof," cried Dridha-Varman; "but lest others should follow their evil example, I will have vengeance on the slanderers. Name them, and their doom shall be indeed a terrible one."

Then Mana Kanaka told the king the whole sad story; and when it was ended the wicked woman who had first thought of injuring the queen, and the barber who had helped her, were sent for to hear their doom, which was—to be shut up for the rest of their lives in prison. This was changed to two years only, because Kadali-Garbha was generous enough to plead for them. As for the third person in the plot, the old witch of the cave, not a word was said about her by anybody. Mana Kanaka knew well enough what her share in the matter had been; but magicians and witches are careful not to make enemies of each other, and so he held his peace.

Dridha-Varman was so grateful to his father-in-law for bringing his wife back to him, that he wanted him to stop at court, and said he would give him a very high position there. But Mana Kanaka refused every reward, declaring that he loved his little home in the forest better than the grand rooms he might have had in the palace. "All I wish for," he said, "is my dear child's happiness. I hope you will never again listen to stories against your wife. If you do, you may be very sure that I shall hear of it; and next time I know that you have been unkind to her I will punish you as you deserve."

The king was obliged to let Mana Kanaka go, but after this he took Kadali-Garbha to see her father in the forest very often. Later, when the queen had some children of her own, their greatest treat was to go to the little home, in the depths of the wood. They too learnt to love animals, and had a great many pets, but none of those pets were kept in cages.